BERLITZ®

KU-775-931

COPENHAGEN

1990/1991 Edition

By the staff of Berlitz Guides

13th Printing
1990/1991 Edition

Updated or revised 1989, 1987, 1986, 1985,
1984, 1982, 1981, 1979

How to use our guide

- All the practical information, hints and tips that you will need before and during the trip start on page 102.
- For general background, see the sections Copenhagen and the Danes, p. 6, and A Brief History, p. 13.
- All the sights to see are listed between pages 23 and 65, with suggestions for day trips from Copenhagen from page 68 to 79. Our own choice of sights most highly recommended is pinpointed by the Berlitz traveller symbol.
- Entertainment, nightlife and all other leisure activities are described between pages 79 and 93, while information on restaurants and cuisine is to be found on pages 94 to 101.
- Finally, there is an index at the back of the book, pp. 126–128.

Found an error or an omission in this Berlitz Guide? Or a change or new feature we should know about? Our editor would be happy to hear from you, and a postcard would do. Be sure to include your name and address, since in appreciation for a useful suggestion, we'd like to send you a free travel guide. Write to: Berlitz Publishing S.A., Avenue d'Ouchy 61, 1000 Lausanne 6, Switzerland.

Although we make every effort to ensure the accuracy of all the information in this book, changes occur incessantly. We cannot therefore take responsibility for facts, prices, addresses and circumstances in general that are constantly subject to alteration.

Text: Vernon Leonard
Photography: Erling Mandelmann. Additional photos courtesy Danish Tourist Board: cover, pp. 52–53 P. Hauerbach; pp. 27, 35 J. Schytte; pp. 41, 42 D. Betz; p. 57 P. Eider; p. 83 M.L. Brimberg
Layout: Doris Haldemann
We would like to thank David Pulman and Margit Storm who helped in the preparation of this guide and, we are also grateful to the Danish Tourist Board and the Tourist Association of Copenhagen for their assistance in this project.
4 Cartography: (Falk) Falk-Verlag, Hamburg

Contents

Cover picture: Nyhavn

Copenhagen and the Danes

Tell a Dane that he's a *hyggelig* man, that his home is *hyggeligt*, even that Copenhagen itself is *hyggelig*, and you'll be saying what he likes to hear.

For *hyggelig* is Denmark's favourite word. Difficult to translate (and almost impossible to pronounce), it means something like warm and cosy. It reflects the Dane's desire to be, not the biggest and best at everything in life (it's only a small country, after all), but the warmest and cosiest of hosts.

Entertaining friends in their homes, surrounded by good furniture and with a beautifully set table well laden with food and drink, is a cherished ideal of Danish life.

So, if the Dane lives it up so much at home, what of outside? You'll soon see he takes no half measures when it comes to entertainment. From the most

Fair heads in a fairy-tale land.
6 *Children enjoying open-air theatre.*

sophisticated night-spot cabarets to cheap back-street sex cinemas it's all there, with a vast choice of bars and restaurants, taverns and pubs, from the formal to... well, just plain *hyggelig*.

But what of these Danes, these latter-day Vikings? Certainly the Dane of today has little to remind one of his ancestors, the pillaging Viking of yore. For one thing he tends to be too wide around the waist from his cakes and cream, lager and aquavit to row small boats across vast seas. He's also the beneficiary (some would say victim) of one of the world's most advanced welfare systems.

Good food is something of a national obsession. The blinding displays of open sandwiches *(smørrebrød)* and some of the world's best pastries *(wienerbrød)* must be seen to be believed. The profusion of delicatessen-type salads, cheeses and fresh fish are as tempting to the eye as to the palate.

As for shopping, some of the finest porcelain, pewter and silver goods are made here, and the concept of functional yet aesthetically pleasing Danish design permeates most things from toys to household appliances.

8

A strong sense of fantasy and colour appears around any corner in Copenhagen. Postmen wear bright red jackets and ride yellow bikes. Chimney-sweeps wear black top-hats, into which they may tuck their lunchtime *smørrebrød*. Buses often drive merrily along with little red-and-white

Danish flags fluttering each side of the driving cab.

A surprisingly ebullient, outgoing people, all in all, for a northern country—a surprising country, too, consisting of no fewer than 406 islands at last count, 97 of them inhabited. Only link with the Continent is the peninsula of Jylland (Jut-

Chocolate-box soldiers change guard daily at Amalienborg Square.

land) that juts up like a finger from northern Germany and dominates the country, in area if not in population. With only five million people, Denmark is still far the most densely populated Scandinavian country (though not the most populous); its 291 people per square mile dwarfs neighbouring Sweden's 46.

Three ice ages have moulded the gently undulating landscape, and the tidy Danes have transformed it into a succession of model farms where barns and farmhouses always seem freshly painted. Grassland and wheatfields sweep down to the roadside, and white medieval churches with distinctive, step-gable towers rise above the village skylines. A few snowy peaks, you might imagine? Denmark's highest hill, Yding Skovhøj, "soars" to a mere 568 feet.

Centre of Danish government, administration and finance, Copenhagen is home to nearly one third of Denmark's five million people. It also lodges the oldest royal dynasty in Europe, now headed by Queen Margrethe II and her French-born husband, Prince Henrik.

Broad highways carve through the 20th-century city. But, off them, Copenhagen still has a well-preserved old-town area of winding cobbled streets, stuccoed houses and curio shops. A quality of fairyland, of magic, pervades the city with its 17th-century green copper roofs and domes, royal legacy of Denmark's great builder-king, Christian IV.

And, crown jewel of this city of pleasure and imagination, the incomparable Tivoli, lying right in the centre of town; more than a funfair, more than a park, it's an institution near to the hearts of all Copenhageners.

Well before Danny Kaye sang it in his song, Copenhagen was known to be "wonderful, wonderful"—a clean, green city of gaiety, culture and charm, with a tradition of tolerance and humour. And the chances are that if Hans Christian Andersen were to return to it, he would still feel at home here today.

Previous page: *montage of a cosy city—park dancing, street meeting, two-wheel mailman, outdoor cafés.* Right: *the pillaging Viking of yore today appears only at festival romp.*

A Brief History

Well before the Vikings had organized themselves into that extraordinary nation of seafarers, Denmark was inhabited by a people of hunters. Prehistoric relics of all kinds, some dating back to 100,000 B.C., abound in Copenhagen's museums and countryside, including Stone Age flint arrow-heads and knives of extraordinary craftsmanship. Bronze Age clothes—blouses and corded skirts for example, the oldest surviving costumes in Europe —have been found, as have musical instruments, including more than 30 examples of the famous Danish *lur*, whose hoarse and sonorous notes seem quite out of tune with the long graceful stem of the instrument itself.

Viking Age

The Vikings appeared at the tail end of the Scandinavian Iron Age (around 800 to nearly

A.D. 1100). At this point, the first written records began to appear. At their peak, these fearless warriors reached Newfoundland, were rounding the North Cape, and making sallies to England, Holland, France, Spain, the Mediterranean, and even as far as the Caspian Sea. Prime examples of their boats can be seen at the Roskilde Viking Ships Museum (see p. 78), and the excavated settlement at Trelleborg in west Zealand shows a camp capable of accommodating 1,300 warriors.

Danish raids into England gathered strength during the late 10th and the first years of the 11th centuries, culminating in a full attempt at conquest. Canute (Knud) the Great, after meeting considerable resistance, won and finally became king of England in 1016. The union was to last until 1042.

Christianity had already been brought to Denmark in A.D. 826 by a Benedictine monk, and received the royal seal of approval when King Harald Bluetooth in 961 was converted by Poppo, another monk, who convinced him by seizing red-hot irons in his bare hands. A runic stone erected by Harald Bluetooth himself at Jelling in East Jutland records that he "won for himself all Denmark and Norway and made the Danes Christians".

Medieval Times

In 1157, Valdemar I, called the Great, came to the throne. He leaned heavily on the influence of Bishop Absalon of Roskilde and this was a partnership of critical importance to Copenhagen, then a little fishing village called Havn. With its fine harbour on the Sound (Øresund in Danish)—that waterway between Denmark and Sweden which forms the main entrance to the Baltic—the village's location on what was becoming one of the main trading routes of medieval Europe destined it to higher things.

Statesman and warrior-hero, Bishop Absalon fortified Havn in 1167 by building a castle on its small harbour island of Slotsholmen; this is now acknowledged to be the founding date of the modern city, and the name Havn in 1170 changed to Køpmannæhafn ("merchants' harbour"), thence to København. Today, Slotsholmen is in the heart of the city. The impressive Christiansborg parliament buildings fill the site, but you can see some remnants of Absalon's castle in their cellars.

In the course of the reigns of successive 12th-century kings,

Denmark sorely over-extended itself in all directions, and was to pay dearly for it in the 13th and 14th centuries. It had interfered in the government of Schleswig and Holstein (the dispute over these two border provinces lasted into the 20th century) and troubled the growing trade of the North German Hanseatic ports. The Germans marched into Jutland. The Danish aristocracy took this opportunity to curb the powers of its monarchy, and in 1282 King Erik V was forced to sign a Great Charter under which he would rule together with the nobles in the Council of the Danish Realm *(Danmarks Riges Råd)*.

But Valdemar IV Atterdag (reigned 1340–75), probably the greatest of medieval Danish kings, now led the country back onto a path of conquests and into conflict with its Nordic neighbours—setting a pattern that was to last intermittently for centuries.

Denmark's hand was greatly strengthened when Valdemar's daughter, Margrete, married Håkon VI, King of Norway and Sweden. After his death, Margrete managed at the Treaty of Kalmar in 1397 to unify the three Nordic powers under her nephew Erik VII of Pomerania. The indomitable Margrete ruled in his name, but died of the plague at the peak of her power in 1412.

After her death, during the true reign of Erik VII (1412–39), Copenhagen was enlarged. The city became official capital under Christopher III of Bavaria in the 1440s; and when a university was founded in 1479 by Christian I, it became the nation's cultural centre, too. By this time, the city's population had grown to about 10,000; Schleswig-Holstein was again under Danish rule; the building of a castle at Helsingør (the Elsinore of Shakespeare's *Hamlet*) had begun, to enforce the payment of Sound tolls, for vital to Denmark's strategic strength at the crossroads of the Northern Seas was control of the Sound. Dues had to be paid by all ships passing through the $2\frac{1}{2}$-mile channel between Helsingør on Zealand and Helsingborg in Sweden—the channel where ferries cross peacefully every few minutes these days. Denmark now stood in a very strong position.

Forests had been cleared, new towns and villages had mushroomed—and the curtain was rising on 200 years marked by civil war against the nobles, the advent of the Lutheran movement in Denmark, and more wars with Sweden. **15**

The Reformation

The latent, deep-seated discontent with abuses within the Catholic Church began—with the vast spread of ideas in the 16th century—to come out into the open. In Denmark itself, Catholic bishops had long been using their wealth to political and military ends, but it was left to Christian III (reigned 1534-59) to break their stranglehold. He declared himself supreme authority of a State Church based on Lutheranism, which, coming from Germany, had made deep inroads. The bishops were imprisoned until they "agreed", and their wealth was used to pay royal debts and train new pastors.

Meanwhile, the Swedish wars grated on disastrously, and fortunes turned in favour of the Danes' adversaries. By the latter half of the 17th century, Denmark had been forced to relinquish her remaining Swedish possessions and to cede the east bank of the Sound to Sweden. This crucial waterway was now forever split down the middle, jointly controlled by the two Scandinavian powers, just as today.

As Denmark licked its many 17th-century war wounds, Copenhagen itself had two great consolations. First, it was made a free city in 1660 in acknowledgement of its bravery during a two-year-long Swedish blockade—which meant in effect that all residents were granted the same privileges as the nobles. Secondly, the earlier part of the century had experienced a wave of new culture and fine building under Christian IV. The "Great Builder", as he was known, had doubled the size of the city by creating, firstly, the Christianshavn area just across the harbour channel on Amager Island as an Amsterdam-like complex of narrow canals, homes and warehouses, and, secondly, building a new housing district (Nyboder) to the north-west of Kongens Nytorv, yellow-wash rows of sailors' houses still standing today. On a grander architectural scale, he was responsible for so many of the monumental green copper roofs that make the Copenhagen skyline uniquely photogenic in the 20th century—among them the Stock Exchange, the Round Tower and the magnificent Rosenborg Castle.

Absolute Power

As a result of the Swedish wars, Denmark went bankrupt and the country was laid waste. Political and social upheaval were both inevitable.

In 1660, King Frederik III matched the mood of the moment and proclaimed himself absolute monarch, thereby depriving the nobles of the Council of the Danish Realm of the powers they had enjoyed more or less continuously since 1282. However, Frederik's absolute rule turned out to be a

Neat rows of yellow-wash sailors' homes at Nyboder erected in 1631–41 by builder-king Christian IV, and still lived in by navy personnel.

period of national unity with a tightly controlled, well-organized central bureaucracy.

The early absolutist kings still waged several costly wars—mainly against Sweden. Copenhagen itself suffered a plague in 1711–12 which killed 22,000 people—or nearly a third of its inhabitants—as well as two devastating fires in 1728 and 1795 which involved major reconstruction of much of the city.

Despite these setbacks, the 18th century was highlighted by major social advancements. Serfdom was abolished in 1788 (note the Freedom Pillar in Vesterbrogade, opposite Central Station), and peasants threw off the yoke of the medieval landlord and worked for themselves. They moved away from the central farmhouse and established their own dwellings and smallholdings in surrounding fields. This gave the Danish countryside its present character of a landscape dotted about with farms, and was of enormous influence in the shaping of modern Denmark.

Round Tower spirals down 700 feet. At nearby Rosenborg Slot, Crown Jewels glisten in the cellar.

Napoleon and the 19th Century

Denmark found itself involved in the European revolutionary wars of the late 18th century without really wanting to. By maintaining their participation in the League of Armed Neutrality along with Russia, Sweden and Prussia to resist Great Britain's claim to the right of searching all vessels at sea, Denmark brought down upon itself the ire of the British. In 1801, a fleet under admirals Nelson and Parker sailed into the bay of Copenhagen. During the ensuing battle, Nelson, so legend would have it, put a telescope to his blind eye to be able to deny having seen a signal to break off the engagement.

Subsequently, Britain, afraid that Napoleon would take over the Dano-Norwegian fleet, demanded its instant surrender. When the Danes refused, Copenhagen was blockaded and in 1807 subjected to a three-day bombardment by the British Navy. Denmark had no choice but to hand over what was left of its fleet to the British, only to be forced immediately afterwards to sign an alliance with Napoleon who was marching fast into Jutland.

When Napoleon was finally brought to his knees, Denmark found itself completely isolated **19** because of this alliance. Norway, where a separatist movement was already strong, was handed over to Sweden in 1814 to pay off war-debts, for Denmark had gone bankrupt. The formerly vast Danish territories overseas were reduced to Greenland, Iceland, the Faroes and the Virgin Islands.

Fifty years later Denmark was to lose the Schleswig and Holstein duchies—a third of its home territory and two-fifths of its population—to Bismarck's Prussia. In the wake of civil turmoil, powdered by the 1848 revolution in France, Frederik VII was forced to relinquish his absolute rule and hand over power to the National Liberal Party.

A liberal constitution was drawn up with wide suffrage, and the Danish "Golden Age" was all set to begin. Søren Kierkegaard had shaken up contemporary philosophy and Christianity with his pioneering existentialism. Bertel Thorvaldsen, the country's greatest sculptor, had returned from Italy and left a profusion of monumental works in Copenhagen. Hans Christian Andersen was strolling the city streets, attending the ballet, reading his fairy-tales to groups of admirers, and rapidly becoming world-famous.

In the city, the old ramparts were demolished. Railroads, factories and workers' housing blocks sprang up, so that by the late 19th century Copenhagen was a thriving industrial centre. In the last quarter of the century, social insurance schemes began to appear—a pioneer development.

Meanwhile in the countryside, much was going on. N.F.S. Grundtvig, a leading European educationalist, had established his system of popular adult high schools in 1844 to improve the peasant's lot, and the first cooperative schemes were afoot.

The 20th Century

In 1901 a landmark was reached in Danish constitutional history when a government was appointed based only on a majority in the lower chamber of parliament *(Folketinget)*. The march of the common people brought them not only into the cities and urban areas, but also into the political strug-

Deep in his bronze dreams, Hans Christian Andersen continues to keep children of all ages amused.

20

gle. Together, in 1915, the Liberal Democrats, Radical Liberals and Social Democrats forced the abolition of electoral privileges in the upper chamber *(Landstinget)* and initiated a system of proportional representation for both chambers. The vote was at last given to women and servants.

The new Danish society was put to severe strain adopting the compromises necessary to maintain neutrality during the First World War. After the war, in a troubled plebiscite, North Schleswig voted itself back permanently into Denmark, and today's border was established.

Industrial unrest, and the severe economic depression between the two world wars, failed to halt Denmark's progress, however. In science, theoretical physicist Niels Bohr of Copenhagen University was making fundamental contributions to atomic research. In architecture, Arne Jacobsen won a competition in 1929 for a circular, sun-rotating "house of the future" capable of accommodating an aircraft on the roof. And in industrial design— furniture-making, cutlery, glass, pewter, silver and textiles— Denmark set new standards, combining utility with beauty, to a point that "Danish design" became synonymous with good, functional and aesthetic articles.

When the Second World War broke out in 1939, the Scandinavian countries issued declarations of neutrality, but on April 9, 1940, Denmark was invaded and collapsed after a token struggle.

The Danish economy, now cut off from the outside world, found itself forced to adapt to the German market, and the country had no choice but to manifest a certain minimum degree of compliance. The anti-Nazi sentiments of the vast majority of Danes were expressed, however, first by "cold-shoulder" treatment, and soon by outright resistance. The Danes managed by different means to smuggle out 7,000 Jews in all to Sweden, out of 7,500 living in the country.

Christian X, the wartime king, became the country's folk-hero as he rode out every day by horse among the crowds. In 1943, the government resigned—it could no longer yield to German demands without losing the support of the population, and the running of the country was left to heads of departments. But the resistance was so organized and well in charge of matters that Denmark was a full member of the Allied forces when the war ended.

So began another era of massive Danish reconstruction, to achieve the society of the latter 20th century—one of the world's most comprehensive and successful attempts at a "welfare state", that has kept its human dimensions. The standard of living—and the quality of life—are among the highest in the Western world.

Politically, Denmark abandoned neutrality when it entered NATO in 1949. Economically, the country was a founder-member of EFTA (the European Free Trade Association), and transferred into the EEC (European Common Market) along with the U.K. and Eire in 1972. It also participated in the postwar revival in Nordic unity by joining the Nordic Council and the Nordic Council of Ministers.

The Dane of today sees his international role as promoting *détente* through the United Nations and other channels. And, steering a deft course through the turbulent currents of modern economic life, the country continues undeterred to work for a just and humane society. The fact that Denmark's influence is felt way beyond its frontiers testifies to the success of its system and to the universal appeal of its aims.

What to See

Rådhuspladsen

Every city has a heart somewhere, and Copenhagen's is doubtlessly Rådhuspladsen (Town Hall Square).

Perhaps 90 per cent of the city sights mentioned in this book lie within a mile of the square. Most planned walks begin, like ours, from Rådhuspladsen, and for wider city excursions, every bus you will need starts here. So do many bus tours of city, countryside, castles and beaches.

Stand with your back to the red-brick Town Hall *(Rådhuset)* on the vast paved area of the Town Hall Square, and watch Danish life stroll and scurry by. Here also is your first hot-dog stand *(pølsevogn)* where tasty Danish sausages are served in a variety of inexpensive forms. The unique Tivoli pleasure gardens are already visible over to your left, just beyond the eight-lane H.C. Andersens Boulevard, where you'll notice at once a very special feature of Danish life—the bicycle. At rush hours, there seem to be millions of them.

The capital's most famous pedestrians-only street is a few **23**

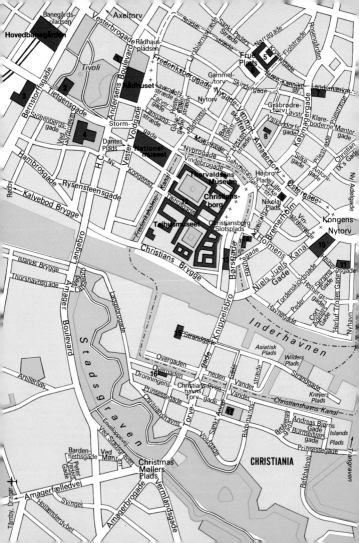

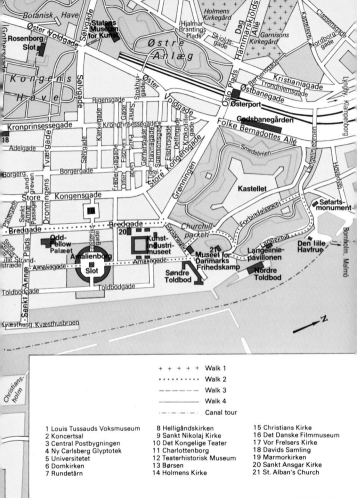

COPENHAGEN – CITY CENTRE

+ + + + + Walk 1
• • • • • • • Walk 2
– – – – – Walk 3
——— Walk 4
——— Canal tour

1 Louis Tussauds Voksmuseum
2 Koncertsal
3 Central Postbygningen
4 Ny Carlsberg Glyptotek
5 Universitetet
6 Domkirken
7 Rundetårn

8 Helligåndskirken
9 Sankt Nikolaj Kirke
10 Det Kongelige Teater
11 Charlottenborg
12 Teaterhistorisk Museum
13 Børsen
14 Holmens Kirke

15 Christians Kirke
16 Det Danske Filmmuseum
17 Vor Frelsers Kirke
18 Davids Samling
19 Marmorkirken
20 Sankt Ansgar Kirke
21 St. Alban's Church

yards to your right. Strøget (pronounced STROY-et), as it is universally known, winds its way for three-quarters of a mile to the city's other main square, Kongens Nytorv, changing name several times on the way and never once officially called Strøget. Other pedestrians-only streets lead off from Strøget, and between them you can satisfy most of your shopping needs with hardly a car in sight.

You'll take in, after a quick sweep of the eye over Rådhuspladsen, some of the statues on this vast open square—a hint of the many hundreds scattered throughout the town, mostly erected by Town Hall or art committees or by the Carlsberg Foundation. Here for a start, on the west corner of the square is the dramatic **Bull-and-Dragon Fountain** (1923) in copper depicting a watery battle between the two beasts.

A few yards away sits a bronze version of Denmark's favourite son, Hans Christian Andersen, brooding by the boulevard that bears his name. For your third quick statue, glance left down Vesterbrogade. Dividing the highway near Central Station is the Freedom Pillar, erected between 1792 and 1797 to commemorate the end of serfdom

Rådhuspladsen, focal point of city life and starting point for visits.

for Danish peasantry in 1788. Next, to your right on Vester Voldgade is a statue that brings a smile to every Dane's face as he tells you about it—the **Lur Blowers Statue.** Local legend

has it that the two ancient men on top will sound a note from their instruments if a virgin ever passes—and though standing on the column since 1914 they've led a life of disconcerting silence.

Turn around now and take a better look at the **Town Hall** itself, built between 1892 and 1905. Its main doorway is crowned by a statue of city founder Bishop Absalon in copper and 22-carat gilt. Above Absalon again, on the roof, stand the rest of our introductory statues—six bronze figures representing nightwatchmen from various periods of the city's history.

Tivoli

Tivoli is magic, and you can't explain magic by statistics. It's an ambiance created by chance and inspiration. You have to see it and feel it to believe it.

It's a reflection of the Dane's desire to have fun in pleasurable surroundings. A place he and his children can enjoy, where his office group can let their hair down, yet where his grandparents can also sit amid the tulips and smoke their daily cigar in peace.

In the heart of the city and on the site of some ancient fortifications, Tivoli's situation as a pleasure park is unique. Visit it by day and in the evening, and you'll find two different worlds. Or stay from 10 a.m. to midnight on the same ticket (costing less than a cinema entry).

It's a hundred thousand flowers blooming at any one time; trees and pathways lit by 110,000 electric light bulbs (no neon), free firework shows three nights a week; and more than 20 snack-bars and restaurants serving anything from hot-dogs to gourmet meals. (There's one restaurant by the lake where you can take your own *smørrebrød* from the Vesterbrogade shops, buy a jug of coffee and be provided with plate, cutlery and napkin, free.)

It's a Chinese pagoda restaurant beside an arcade of rowdy slot machines; a concert hall offering everything from the Berlin Philharmonic to the Århus Fire Brigade Band; some 85 shops; free waltzes and oom-pah-pahs from the bandstand, and merry-go-rounds for the kids; a pantomime theatre; coloured fountains by the lake; and the Tivoli Boy Guard's Band marching through like a scaled-down version of the Queen's Life Guard itself.

Five million people visit privately owned Tivoli each year, equivalent to the entire population of Denmark. Approximately 300 million have paid admission since Georg Carstensen gained a royal licence to operate the site in 1843. The 20-acre pleasure park, equivalent to nine large city blocks, is on lease from Copenhagen Council till 1995. Few fear for its continuance.

Tivoli is open from May 1 to mid-September. A programme of events describing what's on is available on the spot.

Tivoli means something different to everyone; but for all it's fun.

Each section of the Town Hall bears a different style and imprint, but they come together architecturally in the same way as a patchwork quilt. The most impressive are the main hall and banqueting room with their statuary and coats-of-arms—especially the view of the 145-feet long hall from the first-floor colonnade.

The only way to see the Town Hall is by guided tour, and these begin in the entrance hall, each hour for the main tour and each half-hour for Jens Olsen's **World Clock.** Consult the lists there for the current schedules.

But no more time to linger at Rådhuspladsen. If it's a windy day, you'll be feeling a fresh breeze from the harbour and the Sound and Baltic beyond. In fact, the Town Hall stands on the shore-line of centuries ago, and the waves would have been lapping at your feet here, in days gone by. Off we go to explore this fascinating, friendly city; but wear comfortable walking shoes.

We have divided up the sights into four convenient tours numbered from 1 to 4, basically designed for walking, easy to follow on the map on pages 24–25.

Not Chinatown, simply dusk falling over the Tivoli Chinese pagoda.

Walk 1:

The Old Town and Strøget

Crossing at the lights between Rådhuspladsen and Vester Voldgade, turn towards the Lur Blowers Statue (hear any note?) and into the first narrow street on your left, Lavendelstræde. Here you will see typical Danish houses and shops from 1796, the year after the city's second great fire, and a view ahead of the massive masonry and archways of Copenhagen's fourth town hall, built between 1805 and 1815, now the country's principal law courts.

The corner house on your right where you turn into Heste-møllestræde is where Mozart's widow lived with her second husband, a Danish diplomat. Carry on across the next junction into Gåsegade, and here you should notice the gabled houses which have 18th-century hoists at the top—furniture is traditionally hauled up by hoists, instead of being trundled up the narrow interior staircases.

At the end of Gåsegade is a delightful little **square,** a suntrap on good days and with a fountain to cool you down. The square's name, Vandkunsten, means "water artifice", and it's here that Copenhagen's first water pipes were laid.

Cross directly now into Magstræde and go back in time. At Nos. 17 and 19 are two of the city's oldest houses, dating from about 1640. Opposite is one of newest off-beat youth centres: Huset ("the house") has the alternative name in English of "Use It"—and you can. Besides having a jazz club and cinema, folk club, theatre and bars, Huset offers a wealth of advice, brochures and information for young travellers, including how to keep out of trouble—or deal with it if you're in it. The entrance is at Rådhusstræde 13.

Straight ahead now, past some interesting courtyards, into **Gammel Strand** (meaning "old shore"). As its name implies, this is the former edge of the city, and over the present-day canal you get your first glimpse of magnificent, green-roofed Christiansborg —home now of parliament, but formerly a royal palace—built on a small island.

Gammel Strand is a place to pause and prime that camera. It's a fine old waterfront. Over to the far right on Frederiksholms Kanal is the low-arched entrance to the vast **National-museet** (see p. 62). Immediately across the canal is an eye-catching but completely untypical Danish sight: a square-arched, yellow-ochre building with a decorated classical frieze that looks like a national tomb. And that's really what it is—a monument to Denmark's greatest sculptor, Bertel Thorvaldsen. Built between 1839 and 1848, **Thorvaldsens Museum** contains a mass of statuary, and the frieze depicts the sculptor's triumphant return from Rome in 1838 (see also p. 65).

Gammel Strand is one of the two main starting points for canal boat tours (the other being in Nyhavn). See CANAL TOURS, p. 107.

A few yards further along

near Højbro Plads stands the statue of the Fiskerkone (Fishwife), scarf around her head, wraps over her shoulders, wearing a stout apron and clasping a fish in her hand. She looks, in fact, exactly like the women who sit inside their stalls by her side every Tuesday to Friday morning. The statue has been on Gammel Strand only since 1940, but the women have been there for centuries.

Nearby rears the magnificent equestrian **statue of Bishop Absalon.** Copper-green, showing the warrior-priest in chain-mail with axe in hand, the statue makes a most impressive shot against a background of redtiled gable roofs and the soaring copper steeple of Skt. Nikolaj Kirke (St. Nicholas Church), now a café, restaurant and gallery.

Cross Højbro to Christiansborg Slotsplads, the square fronting onto the main entrance of the **Christiansborg complex.**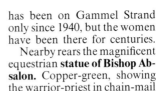

This is the sixth castle or palace on the site since Absalon built his fortress here in 1167, pillage, fire or rebuilding frenzy having taken their subsequent toll. The third castle became the permanent seat of king and government in 1417. The present edifice dates only from the early years of this century when an architectural contest to design the new Christiansborg was won by Thorvald Jørgensen. On November 15, 1907, King Frederik VIII laid a foundation stone hewn from

Cruising past Christiansborg's "back door"—the Marble Bridge. **33**

the granite of Absalon's castle remains. Above this a vast plinth was made of about 7,500 boulders donated by 750 Danish boroughs, and the palace was faced with granite slabs. Look up a little to see 57 masks in granite of the country's greatest men.

Sheathed in copper in 1937–39, the roof of monumental Christiansborg today makes a significant contribution to the city's characteristic green skyline.

Christiansborg's chapel, theatre museum, riding lodges and the lovely, restored **marble bridge,** which managed to survive two disastrous fires in 1794 and 1884, help to give the palace a more venerable aspect than its generally very recent origins might lead one to expect.

The palace's interior holds enough delights to fill a whole day's viewing. See pp. 58–60 for more details.

For the moment, however, we continue further along the canal to the highly ornamented **Børsen** (Stock Exchange) dating from the days of Christian IV. It has (of course) a green copper roof with a famous spire composed of four intricately intertwined dragons' tails. Christian IV was much influenced by the booming Netherlands

architecture of the day, and in 1619 commissioned two Dutch brothers to put up the pleasant, somewhat quaint building that could have stepped straight out of a fairy-tale. Copenhagen's stock exchange has since emigrated to Strøget.

Glance left—across the canal—past the Børsgade street flower market, and see another building rising straight out of the water, Venetian-style but with Dutch gable ends and a small copper tower in the middle. The building was originally a 16th-century anchor forge. Then along came Christian IV in 1619 with his Midas touch as a builder, and transformed it into a sailors' church. **Holmens Kirke** is a real surprise when you walk inside: it's so small and cosy, giving an impression of warmth and wood rather than stone and statuary. On the altar, the reredos and the pulpit, there's a veritable outburst of oak carving by Abel Schrøder the Younger, who would otherwise have been totally unknown today.

Holmens Kirke is a favourite with the Royal Family, and in 1967 Queen Margrethe was married here to Prince Henrik, formerly the French Count de Laborde de Montpezat. It holds a special place in the

Skt. Nikolaj Kirke steeple overlooks the lively, bustling Strøget.

affections of naval men also—the adjoining chapel (added in 1706–08) is dedicated to sea heroes from the 17th-century admiral Baron Niels Juel to Danish sailors who died in the last war.

Two ship models hang from the ceiling of the church, a deep-seated tradition you'll note in many Danish churches.

Up Admiralgade opposite the church, across the Holmens Kanal street, you approach the 230-foot spire of Skt. Nikolaj Kirke which has been coming into view regularly since the fishwives' corner. Destroyed several times by fire, it was rebuilt as recently as 1917 and is no longer used for church services, only for public functions such as art exhibitions.

Walk now along Vingårdsstræde, and you're in an area of jazz clubs, small bars **35**

Walk-street Strøget, winding its way between the city's main squares. Shops, cafés, small bars abound; atmosphere is informal and cheerful.

and artists' dives; carry on to Kongens Nytorv (described on p. 39), and left into the north-east end of **Strøget.**

Strøget is a charming and delightful traffic-free urban island to stroll along, by day or in the evening, with its numerous small bars, pavement cafés and excellent shops. It changes name four times during its ³/₄-mile course. At the Kon-

Amagertorv 6, you'll see a fine example of Dutch baroque, now a famous porcelain showroom. Note, also, the 17th–18th-century Helligånds-kirke (Church of the Holy Ghost) with its grassy square.

Another short stroll now along Strøget. As you pass the end of Hyskenstræde and Bad-stuestræde you're in an area of side-streets well worth further investigation if you're interested in antiques, curios and the off-beat little shop that likes to hide away from the main tourist routes.

Opening out, Strøget again becomes a broad pedestrian area comprising the two squares of Gammeltorv and Nytorv, with another cluster of pavement cafés. On Nytorv, you have a full-frontal view of the simple yet powerful law courts. The **Caritas Fountain** on Gammeltorv is the city's oldest, dating from 1610. It's an annual tradition (dating from the golden wedding of King Christian IX and Queen Louise in 1892) to make imitation golden apples dance on the jets on the monarch's birthday (now April 16).

Strøget now makes its last change of name to Frederiks-berggade, and 200 yards away is our starting point, Rådhus-pladsen.

gens Nytorv end, it begins as Østergade, thence Amagertorv, Vimmelskaftet, Nygade and Frederiksberggade.

On the first stretch, off Ostergade, **Pistolstræde** is a picturesque alley lined with shops and small restaurants from five centuries of Copen-hagen history. Further on at

37

Walk 2:

Kongens Nytorv and the Harbour

This walk starts at **Kongens Nytorv** (buses 1, 6, 28, 29 and 41 from Rådhuspladsen), the "king's new square" of Christian V, laid out around 1680, and still the city's largest square with 12 streets leading off it.

Setting the tone of its eight gracious acres is **Det kongelige Teater** (Danish Royal Theatre) on the south-west side. This is the country's greatest cultural centre, at once the home of Danish national ballet, opera and drama. Originally opened in 1748, and rebuilt in 1874, it was briefly the stage of Hans Christian Andersen, the gauche lad from Odense who tried vainly to become a ballet dancer there.

The house next door, fronting the south side of Nyhavn canal, is said to be the major work of pure baroque remaining in Denmark. Called **Charlottenborg** because Queen Charlotte Amalie lived in the massive edifice from 1700, it has been the seat of the Royal Danish Academy of Art since 1753.

Built between 1672 and 1683 by Frederik III's illegitimate son, Ulrik Frederik Gyldenløve, Charlottenborg was of enormous architectural importance in Denmark. Not only were many country mansions modelled after this red-brick Dutch baroque design by Netherlands' architect Evert Janssen, but Ulrik also made the nobility build alongside him in Kongens Nytorv and develop the square in a manner worthy of its royal name.

Consequently, look around and see some other fine buildings here: **Thotts Palæ** (Thott's Mansion) in the north-east corner, built for the naval hero Admiral Niels Juel and now the French Embassy, and the quaint triangular building between Bredgade and Store Strandstræde, the beautifully preserved 1782 **Kanneworffs Hus.**

Centrepiece of the square is an elaborate equestrian statue of Christian V, with four classical figures seated submissively under his horse.

Now walk across the square towards **Nyhavn,** meaning "new harbour". You'll immediately notice the nautical flavour of this one-time "sailors' street". At this end of the canal, dug into the middle of the city in 1671 to enlarge

Strøget hawker with literary bent.

the harbour facilities, stands a sizeable old anchor, a memorial to the Danish sailors killed in World War II.

Over the centuries the two sides of the canal have developed into a unique picture of old Copenhagen. Much painted and photographed, Nyhavn is now a mixture of taverns and restaurants on the immediate north side, and elsewhere of elegantly restored frontages, luxury apartments, some good restaurants and one superb hotel conversion of an 18th-century warehouse.

Hans Christian Andersen lived twice in Nyhavn, dreaming up fairy-tales at No. 67 from 1854 to 1864 and later residing at No. 18. This is a street with almost everything—history, architecture, night-life, a constant passage of colourful small boats and a terminus for canal-boat tours as well as the hydrofoil service to Sweden.

Walk right down Nyhavn (take the north side) for a fine view across the inner harbour to Christianshavn and the spiralling steeple of Vor Frelsers Kirke (see page 52).

Bear round left to Skt. Annæ Plads, a boulevard of consulates and fine old offices, then right into Amaliegade and through a wooden colonnaded archway into the spacious and stately square of **Amalienborg Palace.** Everything here is in studied symmetry. On four of the eight sides stand four

Nyhavn—a pleasant area in which to drink coffee and sample those delicious cakes.

identical mansion-like palaces. From each one jut two wings. Four roads converge at right-angles on the impressive court-yard and 16 bearskin-topped soldiers guard each palace and corner, plus an extra man at the gateway. The queen lives in the right-hand wing next to the colonnade.

Amalienborg was named after the wife of Frederik III, Queen Sophie Amalie, but the buildings burned down in 1689. The present mansions on the same site were originally de-signed as noblemen's homes by court architect Nicolai Eigtved during a city expansion of the 1750s. After Christians-

Weary walkers rest their feet by the Amaliehaven fountain.

borg castle was again destroyed by fire in 1794, the royal family gradually bought up Amalienborg from the nobles and has lived there ever since. Today it's reckoned to be one of the finest rococo ensembles in Europe. Its centrepiece is a unique copper **equestrian monument** to King Frederik V.

The biggest Amalienborg attraction of all is the **changing of the guard.** At 11.30 each morning, when the queen is in residence, the guards leave their barracks near Rosenborg Castle and march through city backstreets to arrive in the palace square just before noon, moving from sentry-box to sentry-box in a series of foot-stamping ceremonies. Up to 70 guardsmen march in with a full band, black bearskins rippling in the breeze, white striped blue trousers and highly polished boots, and, on special festive occasions, red tunics with neat white shoulder straps.

The popular gardens of **Amalienhaven** lie between Amalienborg Palace and the harbour. Belgian landscape architect Jean Delogne used French limestone and Danish granite, while Italian sculptor

Arnaldo Pomodoro created the bronze pillars around the fountain.

Next stroll north along Amaliegade again to the junction with Esplanaden, where several sights spring to view. **Museet for Danmarks Frihedskamp 1940–45** (the Museum of the Danish Resistance Movement 1940–45; see also p. 62), located in one of the prettiest spots in town—especially at daffodil time—also offers the opportunity for a lunch snack at the cafeteria or simply on the benches outside.

St. Alban's Church, as typical an English church as anything this side of Kent, was in fact put up in 1887 by an English architect amid the green lawns of the Churchill Park.

The sight that will arrest your attention even longer is the **Gefion Fountain,** Copenhagen's most spectacular, erected by the Carlsberg Foundation in 1908 and depicting the legend of the Nordic goddess Gefion, who turned her four sons into oxen and used them to plough the island of Zealand out of Sweden. Sculptor Anders Bundgaard's monument makes dramatic use of a small slope near the church, and as the goddess and her "sons" drive down it, there is a massive spray of water all around.

Follow signposts north now to Langelinie through delightful gardens and past another succession of statues and memorial stones until you arrive at the most famous of them all, the **Little Mermaid** *(Den Lille Havfrue)*. In Andersen's fairy-tale, the tragic sea-girl exchanged her voice for human legs in order to gain the love of an earthly prince, but mutely had to watch as he jilted her for a real princess. In desperation, she threw herself into the sea and turned to foam.

To the consternation of Danes and visitors alike, the mermaid has been vandalized several times. On one occasion her head was sawn off; on another she lost her arm. Luckily, the workshop of sculptor Edvard Eriksen retains the original moulds from 1913, and new parts can be cast as required.

If you have leg-power left, you can continue half a mile to **Langelinie** itself—a colourful quay when the tour ships are in—otherwise divert into the Citadel gardens nearby, before turning homewards.

Kastellet (the Citadel) was a cornerstone of Christian IV's defences of Copenhagen. The 300-year-old fort (built mostly between 1662 and 1725) is still used by the army—the church, prison and main guardhouse have resisted the assaults of time. It is a delightfully peaceful enclave in a modern city, with a charming windmill (1847) and remains of the old ramparts to be seen (as in Tivoli and Ørsteds Park also).

Within walking distance of the Citadel is **Nyboder** (meaning "new dwellings"), erected for his sailors by good King Christian IV between 1631 and 1641. Yellow-painted, with shuttered windows and steep gable roofs, they are a quaint and well-preserved little community of houses, still dwelt in by navy personnel, in the triangle where Øster Voldgade meets Store Kongensgade.

Leave the Citadel garden by the southern exit onto Esplanaden, and turn your steps towards **Bredgade.** From here to Kongens Nytorv is a once-fashionable residential quarter of substantial granite houses and quadrangles, planned by architect Nicolai Eigtved at the same time as Amalienborg. At No. 70, a plaque commemorates the philosopher Søren Kierkegaard's death there in 1855. Next door at No. 68 is Kunstindustrimuseet (Museum of Decorative Art), a fine rococo building and former 18th-century hospital. See page 60–61 for details.

Almost next door again, at No. 64, is Skt. Ansgar Kirke, centre of the city's modest Roman Catholic community since 1842. A museum at the rear of the church traces Catholicism in Copenhagen since its virtual extinction in the Reformation of 1536.

Past two stately mansions on the corner of Fredericiagade, the three golden, onion-shaped domes of the **Alexander Newsky Kirke,** built for the Russian Orthodox community between

Indifferent to stares of canal-trippers, Andersen's forlorn Little Mermaid gazes endlessly out to sea.

1881 and 1883, come into view. Guided tours in five languages are advertised each day except Sunday from 11 a.m. to 2 p.m.

As Bredgade opens out at the junction with Frederiksgade, leading to the Amalienborg Royal Palace, the magnificent dome of **Marmorkirken** (Marble Church) rises high to your right. Some 100 feet in dia-

meter, this is one of the largest church domes in Europe. Planned around 1740 by Nicolai Eigtved to be the centre-point of this new "Frederik's Town" area (the church is also known as *Frederikskirken*), its foundation stone was laid by King Frederik V in 1749 amid great ceremony. However, by 1770 the Norwegian marble required for the building had become so expensive that the project was halted and for a century it remained a picturesque ruin. It was finally consecrated in 1894, Norwegian marble having been complemented by Danish marble from Faxe.

Inside, it's both impressive and beautiful. Carried on 12 stout pillars, the dome is decorated with rich frescoes in blue, gold and green. Blue light filtering through stained glass behind the baroque altar adds yet another original touch of colour. Outside, the church is surrounded at street level by statues of personalities of the Danish Church, from such dignitaries as St. Ansgar (who helped bring Christianity to Denmark) to Grundtvig, the 19th-century

educationalist. On the roof terrace are 16 statues from international religious history ranging from Moses to Luther.

The Marble Church is a rewarding visit and an excellent place to rest awhile before concluding your walk down elegant Bredgade back to Kongens Nytorv.

Old-town roofs from top of Marble Church; old-time interest in books in fascinating university area.

Walk 3:

University Quarter and Parks

Head west this time from Rådhuspladsen a short way along Vester Voldgade and turn right into narrow Studiestræde, with its motley collection of antique shops, bookstalls and boutiques in an 18th-century setting.

Almost at the end of Studiestræde, at No. 6, a plaque records that H.C. Ørsted, discoverer of electro-magnetism in 1820, lived here. And a few yards further on, at the corner of Nørregade, you'll see one of Copenhagen's oldest preserved buildings, the 1500 former **Bispegården** (Bishop's Residence), now part of the University. On Bispetorvet stands the 1943 monument commemorating the 400th anniversary of the introduction of the Reformation to Denmark. Over the square looms the sombre Cathedral *(Domkirken)* of Copenhagen, called **Vor Frue Kirke** (Church of Our Lady). Bishop Absalon's successor, Sunesen, is said to have laid its foundations in the 12th century, but by 1316 it had already burned down four times. Two later constructions were also destroyed—by the great 1728

fire and by British bombardment in 1807. Following this, the present church was reconstructed by V.F.K. and C.F. Hansen in 1811–29.

Its large austere interior is relieved by a heroic collection of statues by Bertel Thorvaldsen; twelve huge marble Apostles line the aisle, and the orange-lit altar is surrounded by bronze candelabra and dominated by Thorvaldsen's famous **figure of Christ.**

The main university block to the north of the Cathedral dates in its present form from the 1830s only, though the University itself was founded in 1479. The area is full of student ambiance, with sidewalk and cellar cafés and fascinating little bookshops.

Behind the Cathedral and the University runs Fiolstræde, a delightful pedestrians-only street. On the corner of Krystalgade stands Copenhagen's Synagogue, inaugurated in 1833.

Retrace your steps back down Fiolstræde, and make the detour into Skindergade, where you'll find **Gråbrødretorv,** a picturesque square of brightly painted 18th-century houses which was the site of a Franciscan monastery until the Reformation. Cafés have proliferated here in recent years;

it's a good place for a break.

Walking towards Købmagergade first by Lille Kannikestræde, then right along Store Kannikestræde, take a look into the exquisite courtyard at No. 10. Admiral Ove Gjedde built this timbered mansion in 1637, dutifully echoing King Christian IV's wish that Copenhagen's beauty should be a joy forever.

The pleasant walking-street of **Købmagergade** is one of Copenhagen's oldest commercial thoroughfares. It's another street with Christian IV overtones, for the ubiquitous builder laid the foundation stone here of Trinitatis Kirke (Trinity Church) in 1637 and built the integral **Rundetårn** (Round Tower) in 1642 as an astronomical observatory. The Round Tower has been one of the city's most beloved landmarks for 300 years, even if it only reaches the modest height of 115 feet. It is more interesting to visit than the rather conventional church itself. You can walk to the top, but not by steps—these would have been impractical for raising the heavy equipment needed there. Instead, a wide spiral-sloping causeway winds its way round for almost 700 feet inside the tower. Not only did Czar Peter the Great ride up it on horse-back in 1716—his empress followed in a coach-and-six.

The tower is open from 10 a.m. to 5 p.m., Monday to Saturday, and from noon to 4 p.m. on Sundays from April to end-October; the rest of the year from 11 a.m. to 4 p.m., Monday to Saturday, from noon to 4 p.m. on Sundays. The observatory is usually open from 8 to 10 p.m. on clear evenings, mid-August–end-April.

Students have lived in the Regensen university hostel, opposite the Round Tower, since 1623. Today it's mainly 18th-century with a notable arcade added in 1909.

One art attraction worth a visit while in this area is the **Musikhistorisk Museum** (Musical History Museum) at Åbenrå 32–34 which has a fine collection of old instruments and musical literature. Don't forget either **Davids Samling** (David Collection) at Kronprinsessegade 30 (see p. 60).

The street called Landemærket beside the Round Tower leads on to the main road, Gothersgade, and a wide expanse of parkland and botanical gardens, as well as one of the most appealing castles to be found in a city anywhere. Directly opposite Landemærket is the **Kongens Have** **49** park, laid out in 1606–07 when Christian IV announced that Christiansborg Palace was becoming too official and oppressive. At the same time, he began to build a small country

mansion for himself in a corner of the site (it was then beyond the town walls) and expanded it eventually into **Rosenborg Slot** (Castle), since 1833 a royal museum of great atmosphere and grace (see p. 64). Christian himself helped to plan the three-storey brick building in Dutch/Danish Renaissance

Summer magic—open-air spectacle in picturesque Gråbrødretorv.

style. This is the cosiest castle you could wish to meet. It has all the frills and furbelows, the turrets and towers, moats and battlemented gateways of a "proper" castle, yet it retains an atmosphere of a weekend retreat.

Gardeners of whatever kidney will want to explore the

Botanisk Have (Botanical Gardens) opposite Rosenborg; and the **Statens Museum for Kunst** (Royal Fine Arts Museum) further north along Øster Voldgade is bound to interest art lovers. For details, see pp. 86 and 64–65 respectively.

From here, bus No. 10 will take you to Kongens Nytorv and 75E (rush hours) will transport you back to Rådhuspladsen.

Walk 4:

Christianshavn

Though there's so much to see within a small radius of Rådhuspladsen and Kongens Nytorv, it's easy and worthwhile to spend a few hours just the other side of the harbour channel, over the bridges Langebro and Knippelsbro in **Christianshavn,** and even to continue to the Amager villages of Store Magleby and Dragør.

The name Christianshavn, meaning Christian's Harbour, is derived—once again—from King Christian IV, and the whole area looks just like a slice of Amsterdam, reflecting Christian's predilection for Netherlands architecture.

Take buses Nos. 2 or 8 from Rådhuspladsen to the square **51**

northeastwards up **Overgaden oven Vandet** to see the Dutch-style warehouses, the narrow houses and small bars, all topped by hoists, and a canal scene of multi-coloured boats.

Turn the corner to the right into Skt. Annæ Gade, and in further contrast a Danish-

Italian sight will meet you —**Vor Frelsers Kirke** (Our Saviour's Church). This brick and sandstone church was built between 1682 and 1696 under the direction of Lambert van Haven. The distinctive spire, with a staircase spiralling outside the structure, was added more than half a century

Copenhagen—as the crow spies.

later by Lauridz de Thurah, said to have been influenced by the Sant'Ivo alla Sapienza church in Rome. A total of 400 steps (a third of them on the outside) lead from the church's entrance to the gilt globe and Christ figure on top of the spire, though you'll be allowed the rare experience of this outdoor climb—if you dare take it—only in good weather.

Copenhageners like to recount that de Thurah made a mistake by designing the spiral **53** the wrong way round, and threw himself from the top when he realized it. The spire was completed in 1752, however, and the records state quite firmly that he lived on another seven years.

The inside of the church is unique. Not simply because of the choir screen guarded by six wooden angels, nor because of the highly ornate white marble font, supported by four cherubs, nor even because of the 1732 altar, replete with allegorical statues and with Dresden-like figures playing in the clouds. The interior is, in fact, crowned by a monumental organ, first built in 1690 and several times remodelled, for the last time in 1965. Beautifully ornamented, its façade embellished with wood-carving, the whole construction is supported by two large stucco elephants.

Elephants are a recurring theme in Denmark, perhaps traceable to the country's oldest order of chivalry, the Order of the Elephant. The central vault of the church is decorated with a crowned monogram of Christian V, together with the royal coat-of-arms and a chain of the Order of the Elephant.

Our Saviour's is open from 9 a.m. to 3.30 or 4.30 p.m. Monday to Saturday, from noon on Sundays (hours are shorter in winter). There's a small charge to climb the tower (closed in bad weather). From the top you have a view out over the city.

Now retrace your steps along Skt. Annæ Gade, cross the bridge and walk to the junction with **Strandgade** facing the Foreign Ministry. This area is a curious mixture of old and new. The Danish Centre for Architecture, a former warehouse at Gammel Dok, is a good example well worth visiting. Turning left into this street of 17th- and 18th-century houses, don't be content with the façades—take a peep into the cobbled courtyards, flanked by numerous small living annexes. N.F.S. Grundtvig spent some years at No. 4B. At No. 6 lived Admiral Peter Wessel Tordenskjold in the early 18th century—a Dano-Norwegian hero who won battles at sea but whose exuberant lifestyle ashore lost him many good neighbours. It's said that every time he called *skål* during his frequent banquets, a salute would be fired from two cannons at the main doorway—and there were many sleepless nights until he was killed in a duel in 1720.

The sombre Christians Kirke across Torvegade blocks the

end of Strandgade. Built in 1755 by Nicolai Eigtved, it has an unexpected interior layout, with arched galleries somewhat reminiscent of an old-time music-hall.

The nearby Knippelsbro will bring you back towards the centre of town, but there's also an option to see some of Amager island and a quaint village by the sea.

Outlying Sights

Public transport takes you beyond the city centre, into suburban Copenhagen. To reach the municipalities of Amager island, to the south, catch a 31 bus at Christianshavns Torv, and after about a mile change either to a No. 30 at Amager Boulevard or to a No. 33 at Sundholmsvej. You now drive through a large housing district that was marshland or allotment gardens only a few years ago, and leave the airport route (passing under the main runway) to reach the village of **Store Magleby,** untouched by time—except for the commotion of Copenhagen Airport.

Here on the village street, in an old farmhouse, is **Amagermuseet** (the Amager Museum), laid out in olden

style, complete with furniture, bedrooms and kitchen. The collection, begun in 1901, was donated by villagers from the surrounding area. In its totally unsophisticated manner the museum explains why this area is so Dutch in atmosphere.

The Dutch connection began when King Christian II (reigned 1513–23) invited a colony of Netherlands farmers to improve soil cultivation in the area and provide the royal table with "as many roots and onions as are needed". He gave the Dutch special privileges to live independently in Store Magleby, which for centuries was known as Hollænderbyen (Dutchmen's Town). They had their own judicial system and church (with services in Dutch or Low German only), and developed a bizarre local costume—a mixture of Dutch, Danish and flamboyant French —a large collection of which is on display at the museum.

The Amager Museum is open from 11 a.m. to 3 p.m. Wednesday to Sunday, June 1–August 31, and, for the rest of the year, on Wednesdays and Sundays only, during the same hours.

Again, hop aboard a 30 or 33 bus for another 1½ miles to the water's edge at **Dragør,** where the harbour is packed with small boats and the 18th-century village is remarkably preserved. A maze of cobbled streets and alleyways leads off from the village's only traffic road. You can walk around completely undisturbed between yellow-wash buildings and postage-stamp gardens and get a vivid impression of what life was like before the internal combustion engine.

Beside the harbour, a 1682 fisherman's cottage (the oldest house in the town) has been converted into the **Dragør Museum,** devoted to local seafaring history—open from 2 to 5 p.m. Tuesday to Friday and from noon to 6 p.m. on Saturdays and Sundays (closed Monday), May 1–Sept. 30 only.

From here, the 30 or 33 bus will take you back to Rådhuspladsen.

This same square is the starting point for a jaunt to **Grundtvig's Memorial Church** on Bispebjerg in north-west Copenhagen. Here, only a 10-minute ride from the centre (buses Nos. 16 and 19 from Rådhuspladsen), six million bricks have been laid as a monument to the man once called Denmark's greatest son.

Nikolai Frederik Severin Grundtvig (1783–1872), founder of the Danish people's high school, was a famed edu-

cationalist, an austere parson and prolific hymn-writer.

Grundtvigs Kirke is also a monument to early 20-century Danish architecture. Its design by Peder Jensen-Klint is stunningly simple but effective in conception and sheer size. A few chosen masons, some of them employed from start to finish, carried through the project that lasted from 1921 to 1940. Everything is in pale-yellow brick—the 160-foot tower and the vaults of the

Young visitors blend into the 200-year-old village of Dragør.

72-foot high nave, all the stairs and pillars, the balustrades, altar and pulpit.

The stainless steel organ pipes (4,800 of them) look down on a vast, uncluttered nave and, indeed, the façade of the cathedral-like building itself is strongly reminiscent of an organ. It's a fitting tribute to a man who composed 1,400 hymns, and a national monument not be missed.

Visiting hours: 9 a.m.–4.45 p.m., Monday to Saturday. Sundays and public holidays from noon to 4 p.m. from mid-May to mid-September, till 1 p.m. the rest of the year.

Museums

Hours are subject to rapid change, and there's little consistency in admission charges. Some museums are free, many cost only a few kroner, but others—particularly the larger castle exhibitions and establishments away from Copenhagen itself—charge quite a lot. Reductions for children are always available, varying between 50 and 80 per cent; they sometimes even get in free. To avoid disappointments, check on opening hours and bus lines before going.

Christiansborg Slot (Christiansborg Castle). The castle is today home of government ministries and Parliament, the Danish Supreme Court, and the centre of a complex of museums, described below.

De Kongelige Repræsentationslokaler (Royal Reception Chambers). A fine starting point, but you must join a conducted tour. This is a no-touch, look-only museum with rules to be observed. First, take off your shoes in the entrance hall and don the canvas slippers provided, for on your route you'll be treading on priceless parquet floors.

Immediately comes the guide's first anecdote: "Look at the roof here, held by epic pillars in the shape of male statues, heads bent to take the weight—a symbol of modern Danes paying their taxes …"

Upstairs are a series of linked rooms in everything from imitation marble to the richly tapestried, gold and green room where monarchs are proclaimed from the balcony overlooking the Castle Square (*Slotspladsen*) below. (Danish monarchs have not been crowned since Christian VIII, but a crowd of 50,000 saw the proclamation of the present Queen Margrethe II in 1972.)

Conducted tours: June–end-Aug.: at 2 p.m., Tuesday to Sunday; Sept.–end-May: at 2 p.m., Tuesday to Friday and Sunday.

Conducted tours, also, of the Parliament *(Folketinget)* and conference chambers: Jan. 1–Dec. 1, Sunday every full hour from 10 a.m. to 4 p.m.; June–Sept., daily from 10 a.m. to 4 p.m., except Saturdays.

Teaterhistorisk Museum (Theatre Museum). Cross the royal riding grounds at the rear of Christiansborg—a scene dominated by a copper equestrian statue of Christian IX—and in an elegant little terrace above the stables is one of the world's most unusual theatre museums. Unusual, for a start, because of the constant aroma of horses seeping up through the 200-year-old creaky floorboards, and it has always been thus. Already at the former Court Theatre's first production in 1767, the authentic country smell was remarked on.

The small auditorium and galleries are packed with Danish and international theatre relics—memorabilia of Hans Christian Andersen, Anna Pavlova, Ibsen; playbills, costumes, prints and photographs of Danish theatre history.

Hours: 2 to 4 p.m. on Wednesdays, Fridays and Sundays (June 1–Sept. 30); no Friday opening in winter.

Tøjhusmuseet (Royal Arsenal Museum). Attendants in three-cornered hats and knee-length red jackets greet you in

Tourists admire the parquet and chandeliered glory of Christiansborg's ornate reception chambers.

this vast building on the south-east side of Christiansborg. It's appropriate for a museum housing one of Europe's most important collections of military uniforms and historic equipment.

In this vast museum, everything is laid out open-plan, very little in glass cases. Cannon balls are piled high like potato stacks. Guns range from a 15th-century cannon of Queen Margrete I's time to sophisticated modern weapons. Three old military planes from 1909, 1921 and 1925 are suspended from the roof.

Upstairs is a glittering display of uniforms and small arms.

Hours: May 1–Sept. 30: 1–4 p.m. weekdays, 10 a.m.–4 p.m. on Sundays; winter: 1–3 p.m. weekdays, 11 a.m.–4 p.m. on Sundays. Closed on Mondays.

Location: Christiansborg Slotsplads.

Buses: 1, 2, 6 and 8 from Rådhuspladsen.

Davids Samling (David's Art Collection). European fine arts from the 17th and 18th century and Persian medieval art, ceramics and Danish silverware of the 18th century housed in a lovely town-house.

Location: Kronprinsesse-gade 30.

Hours: 1–4 p.m. every day except Monday, all year round.

Buses: 7, 10 and 17 from Kongens Nytorv.

Den Hirschsprungske Samling (The Hirschsprung Collection). A charming little museum devoted to 19th-century Danish painting, sculpture and decorative art. At the turn of the century, Heinrich Hirschsprung, a rich tobacco merchant, donated the works to the Danish state. Look out for the portraits and pristine landscapes of C.W. Eckersberg (1783–1853), a teacher at Copenhagen's Royal Academy, whose meticulous style had a far-reaching influence. Johan Lundbye's romantic landscapes date from mid-century. A generation later, Peter Severin Krøyer popularized social realist themes, while Laurits Tuxen developed a unique Impressionist style as a student in Paris.

Location: Stockholmsgade 20.

Hours: Daily 1–4 p.m. Also open Wednesday evenings 7–10 p.m. (Closed on Mondays and Tuesdays.)

Kunstindustrimuseet (Museum of Decorative Art). A large display of European and Oriental

handicrafts from the Middle Ages in 1757 rococo buildings.
Location: Bredgade 68.
Hours: May 1 to Sept. 30: 10 a.m.–4 p.m. Tuesday to Sunday; Oct. 1 to April 30: 1–4 p.m. Tuesday to Sunday.
Buses: 1 and 6 from Rådhuspladsen.

Københavns Bymuseum & Søren Kierkegaard Samling (Copenhagen City Museum and Søren Kierkegaard Collection). Founded in 1901, this museum is a children's favourite with its scale model of the city centre (1525–1550) in its front garden. Inside are exhibits of signboards and clothing, building fragments, photographs, engravings and posters from the city's past.

There also is a small collection devoted to the influential 19th-century Danish philosopher Søren Kierkegaard.
Location: Vesterbrogade 59.
Hours: Apr. 1–Oct. 31: daily 10 a.m.–4 p.m.; winter: 1–4 p.m. (closed Mondays); also 7–9 p.m. all year round on Tuesdays.
Buses: 6, 16, 28 and 41 from Rådhuspladsen.

Legetøjsmuseet (Toy Museum). Interesting display of our grandparents' toys, from handmade to mechanical.

Location: Valkendorfsgade 13.
Hours: All year round: 10 a.m. to 4 p.m. daily
Buses: 1, 6, 28 and 41 from Rådhuspladsen.

Louis Tussauds Voksmuseum (Louis Tussaud's Wax Museum). Wax models of famous Danish and foreign personalities.
Location: H.C. Andersens Boulevard 22, 100 yards from Rådhuspladsen.
Hours: May to mid-Sept.: 10 a.m. to midnight daily; mid-Sept. to end-April: 10 a.m. to 4.30 p.m. daily.

Museet for Danmarks Frihedskamp 1940–45 (Museum of the Danish Resistance Movement 1940–45). A graphic record of wartime tragedy and eventual triumph. Every half hour or so, a loudspeaker commentary in Danish and English guides you round the pictures and exhibits.
Location: Churchillparken.
Hours: May 1 to Sept. 15: 10 a.m.–4 p.m. Tuesday to Sunday; Sept. 16 to April 30: 10 a.m.–5 p.m. Tuesday to Sunday.
Buses: 1 and 6 from Rådhuspladsen.

Nationalmuseet (National Museum). This is nothing less **61**

than a well-organized labyrinth of artefacts from Stone Age Danish rock carvings to Mongolian tents and horse-riding equipment. The biggest museum in Scandinavia, it holds an uncountable number of exhibits in eight separate major collections, ranging from prehistoric to Middle Ages, town and manor culture, ethnographical, special and classical antiquity, coins and medals. Many have varying opening hours, so visits must be carefully planned; check first.

Visitors will be intrigued to see the prehistoric Denmark that led up to those extraordinary Viking times. Outstanding among Stone Age exhibits is the Hindsgavle Dagger (1800–1500 B.C.), fashioned from flint in careful imitation of the bronze weapons already in use elsewhere. Bronze technology came to Denmark sometime after 1500 B.C., and a wealth of interesting objects of the period are on view. The most striking exhibit is the Sun Chariot of 1200 B.C. For the Danes, who worshipped the sun, imagined it just as it's depicted here: a disc of gold riding through the sky in a chariot, pulled along by a celestial horse.

Through its colonization of Greenland, Denmark can also open doors to Eskimo culture. There's a lively exhibition (ground floor rooms, Ny Vestergade entrance) of huskies, igloos, reconstructed Eskimo camps, and of medieval clothes preserved in the Greenland subsoil.

Location: Frederiksholms Kanal 12/Ny Vestergade 10.

Hours: Varied, consult lists.

Buses: 1, 2 and 6 from Rådhuspladsen.

Ny Carlsberg Glyptotek (Glyptotek Museum). A split personality museum with a touch of genius at either end of the psychic range. Basically, the Glyptotek was founded on the classical collection of Carl Jacobsen, Danish brewer and art connoisseur (1842–1914), and developed by his family. Today, under one elaborate roof, you can thus see one of the world's foremost exhibitions of Egyptian, Greek, Roman and Etruscan art, with enough statues and artefacts to equip 100 ancient temples. As the museum was specially built around the classical collection, you get unique features like

Brewer's dream brought classical splendours to Glyptotek Museum.

the breathtaking central hall, which appears to have been transplanted direct from ancient Rome.

Other side of the picture: 25 Gauguins, three van Goghs, several Monets and seven Rodin statues competing for attention in a compressed, four-room show, with a complete set of Degas bronzes—73 delicate little statues that won the painter posthumous acclaim as a sculptor.

Location: Dantes Plads, on H.C. Andersens Boulevard, around 300 yards from Rådhuspladsen.

Hours: 10 a.m.–4 p.m. daily from May 1 to Aug. 31; winter: noon–3 p.m. weekdays, 10 a.m.–4 p.m. on Sundays (closed Monday all year round).

Rosenborg Slot (Rosenborg Castle). The castle's 10,000 exhibits span Danish royal history over the past 300 years, but apart from the dazzling cellar display of crown jewels, the emphasis of interest lies on the relics from founder Christian IV himself.

The castle's 24 rooms are arranged chronologically and begin with his tower room study, in essence still furnished in original style. Arrows point your route around the castle, and an excellent official guide

is available in several languages. The Knight's Hall should not be hurried, with its Swedish Wars tapestries, ornately decorated ceiling and three almost life-size silver lions. In the hall is also one of the world's largest collections of silver furniture, mainly 18th century.

The treasury in the cellar contains the crown jewels. Beside the oldest existing specimen of the Order of the Elephant (from about 1580) are 18 cases of crowns, gilded swords, precious stones and coronation cups—even royal inkwells and tea-sets in pure gold; centrepiece of the room is the 17th-century crown of the absolute monarchy—gold, with diamonds, two sapphires and ruby spinels.

Location: Øster Voldgade 4 A.

Hours: May 1 to circa end-Oct.: daily, 11 a.m.–3 p.m.; winter: Tuesday and Friday, 11 a.m.–1 p.m., Sunday 11 a.m.–2 p.m. In June, July and August, the museum opens at 10 a.m.

Buses: 14 and 16 from Rådhuspladsen, or S-train to Nørreport.

Statens Museum for Kunst (Royal Museum of Fine Arts). Here is a finely presented display of paintings from early

Netherlands to modern Danish in a light, airy building. The museum is particularly strong on 19th-century Danish landscapes, Matisse, representative Dutch and Flemish works from Rembrandt to Paulus Potter, an Italian collection including Titian and Tintoretto; and perhaps the world's finest collection of Dürer prints.

In the Danish collection, note Niels Larsen Stevns (1864–1941), one of the great painters of his day, whose bold colours dramatized works ranging from religious themes to scenes from the life of H.C. Andersen. The troll-like grotesques of the German expressionist Emil Nolde (1867–1956) will also catch the eye.

Location: Corner of Sølvgade and Øster Voldgade.

Hours: 10 a.m.–5 p.m. every day of the year except on Mondays.

Bus: 10 from Kongens Nytorv and 75E (rush hours) from Rådhuspladsen.

Thorvaldsens Museum. This is another museum of classical intent. The Roman and Greek gods and goddesses gazing down at you in profusion here, however, are all 19th-century revivals of antiquity—the life's work of Bertel Thorvaldsen (1770–1844), Denmark's greatest sculptor and Copenhagen's only honorary citizen.

Returning home after 40 years in Rome—the Danish government brought him back in triumph—he devoted his collection, library and fortune to the creation of a museum of his own works and chose a young architect, Gottlieb Bindesbøll, to design it. The result was one of Copenhagen's most distinctive and untraditional buildings, with a decorated ochre façade and strong colours everywhere inside—walls and ceilings in black, reds, blues and oranges, which throw into high contrast the pure white marble and plaster of Thorvaldsen's sculpture.

The ground-floor exhibition in 21 interlinked sections is proof before your eyes of why he has been called one of the greatest sculptors since the days of the Caesars—a noble array of chaste classic gods, popes and aristocracy, an idealized vision of mankind with never a wart in sight.

Location: Slotsholmen.

Hours: May 1 to Oct. 31: 10 a.m.–4 p.m. Tuesday to Sunday; Nov. 1 to April 30: 10 a.m.–3 p.m. Wednesday to Sunday.

Buses: 1, 2 and 6 from Rådhuspladsen.

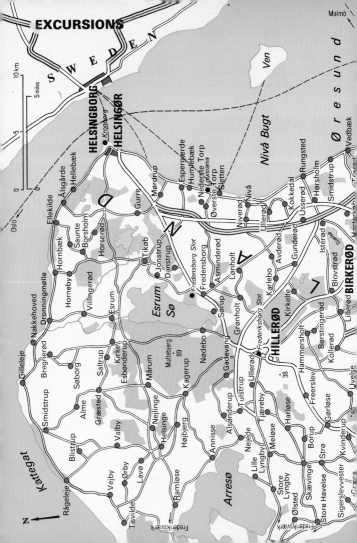

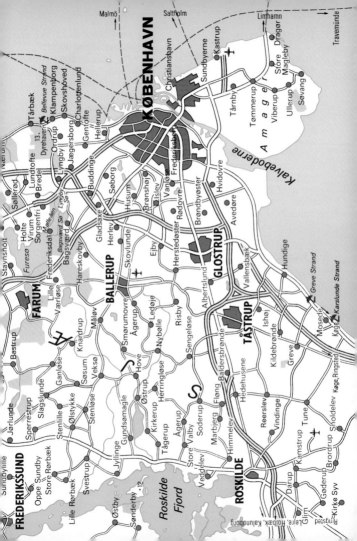

Excursions

In a country of 17,000 square miles, nature has ingeniously split Denmark into more than 400 islands so that you are never more than 30 miles from the sea. Copenhageners even have their own beach, woodlands and wide lake area, and it's possible within the city boundary to organize an excursion including a boat-trip, windmills and water-mills, a royal country castle and genuine village settings.

Open-Air Folk Museum and Lyngby Lake

Initially we're aiming for Frilandsmuseet (Open-Air Folk Museum) at Sorgenfri, 13 km. north of the city centre, accessible by car along the A3 and A5 main roads, by direct bus 84 from Nørreport terminus in town, or by S-train, line A or Cc to Sorgenfri station. A more interesting and adventurous route is to take the same train and change at Jægersborg station to the little red one-coach train called *Grisen* ("The Pig")—from the sound, of its predecessor's whistle —which will drop you off at Fuglevad Station near the back entrance of the museum.

Forty farmhouses, cottages, workshops (and a Dutch-type windmill) are sprinkled through the 90-acre site of **Frilandsmuseet.** All the buildings are furnished in strictly authentic style, with everything down to combs and family portraits lying around.

Broadly, the buildings are divided into geographic groups laid out along country lanes, with old bridges and village pumps, and authentically landscaped. Every one has been transplanted, timber by timber, tile by tile, from its original location. There is a Zealand group, a Jutland and a Faroes group, etc. Homes of all classes are represented, from peasant to landowner through artisan and farmer: you can see graphically how they all lived.

The smell of old timber and tar pervades the rooms. Geese and sheep are driven along the lanes. Displays of folk dancing, sheep shearing, threshing and weaving are given during the summer. There are horse-and-carriage rides, and picnic spots in tree-lined meadows.

Since both opening hours and times of guided tours (in English) tend to change from one year to the next, refer to the daily press or the Copenhagen

Tourist Board office (see p. 124).

Leave yourself time on a fine day to stroll half a mile down the main road towards LYNGBY and a rural boat ride hardly equalled in any capital city. Note, on your left, the white-walled, baroque castle, **Sorgenfri Slot,** built in the 18th century by Lauridz de Thurah, the

At Open-Air Folk Museum, each house is transplanted integrally from its original old-time setting.

same man who designed the spiralling spire of Vor Frelsers Kirke (see p. 52). Under the road then passes Mølleåen (the Mill Stream).

Now follow signs to the right saying *Lyngby Sø—Bådfarten* ("Lyngby Lake—Boat-Trip") and you'll soon be greeted at the quayside by two venerable canopied boats that have been plying the four local lakes since the 1890s.

A 45-minute **cruise** Lyngby-Frederiksdal or Lyngby-

Sophienholm will give you the flavour of these delightful tree-covered backwaters and broad reedy lakes. The boats operate from May to September or October, depending on the weather.

As you float by, you'll pass the 1803 mansion of Marienborg amid the trees, official summer residence of Danish prime ministers; further on lies Frederiksdal with its **castle** on a hill above. This former royal house has been lived in by the same family since 1740.

The alternative trip takes you to **Sophienholm Mansion** (1805), now a community art and cultural centre with outdoor café tables giving an idyllic view over the waters of Bagsværd Sø.

Back on Lyngby quay, the 84 bus will take you direct to town again, or it's a short walk to Lyngby S-train station to rejoin the A- or Cc-line service.

North Zealand and its Castles

Some 70–80 miles of sea views and castle turrets, beaches and rolling farmland—this is what to expect as you tour northern Zealand.

In fine weather you might prefer the lovely drive through the beach suburbs north of Copenhagen and along the so-called Danish Riviera, with its small fishing villages and bays. If it's not exactly seaside weather, or if you're pushed for time, head straight up the A3 motorway (expressway) out of Copenhagen in the direction of Helsingør.

A major attraction just south of HUMLEBÆK, accessible from either the A3 or the coast road, is the **Louisiana Modern Art Museum,** housed in the mid-19th-century mansion of a thrice-married cheese merchant all of whose wives were called Louise. The superb gardens are now dotted with sculptures ranging from chunky Henry Moores to sharp metal constructions by Alexander Calder. The airy, white interior houses anything from mural-sized Chagalls to special pop-art shows (open 10 a.m. to 5 p.m. all year round).

The **castle** at **Helsingør** (which we know better as Elsinore) soon comes into view now, jutting out towards Sweden, a striking square of green roofs against the blue Sound.

"Hamlet's castle" is, of course, a misnomer. Though Laurence Olivier and Vivian Leigh certainly trod its ancient corridors when making the

Hamlet film, the tragic prince himself never slept nor saw a ghost here, and Shakespeare probably derived the name from Amleth (or Amled), a Jutland prince of pre-Viking times.

The castle's real name is Kronborg, and it was built between 1574 and 1585 at the command of King Frederik II. Its purpose was to help extract tolls from ships entering the narrow Sound (and thus the Baltic) at this point.

But Frederik had more than a stronghold in mind. He built a castle that could be lived in, so fortified with high ramparts and massive bastions that large windows and decorated towers and spires could be added with impunity. He sent for Flemish architect Antonius van Opbergen to design the four-wing structure and engaged Danish and Dutch artists to paint, weave tapestries and indulge in decorative sculpture on a scale never before seen in Scandinavia.

Restored this century, the moated brick castle stands today as Frederik's proudest memorial, now sparsely furnished but immensely impressive. It has the feel of solid strength and royal presence, permeating the elaborate little **chapel,** the long galleries and stone stairways, and above all the huge oak-beamed **Banqueting Hall.** At 210 feet by 36, it is the largest hall of its kind in northern Europe and one of the noblest rooms of the Danish Renaissance. Now decked with 12 allegorical paintings of the Sound by Isaac Isaacsz, its white-washed walls were originally hung with 42 famous tapestries by the Dutchman Hans Knieper, portraying the 111 Danish kings said to have reigned before Frederik II. Fourteen of the tapestries survive, seven now hung in a small room beneath the hall and the others in the National Museum in Copenhagen.

The interesting **Handels- og Søfartsmuseum** (Trade and Maritime Museum) in the castle's northern wing contains an exhibition of old navigation instruments as well as relics from early Danish settlements in Greenland and elsewhere.

The castle is open every day all year round: May–Sept.: 10 a.m.–5 p.m.; Nov.–March: 11 a.m.–3 p.m.; April and October: 11 a.m.–4 p.m. Guided tours every half-hour.

After stopping, perhaps, for a coffee at one of the several cafés on Helsingør's 18th-century market place, we now continue along the northern coast road to DRONNINGMØLLE, which has one of the best beaches on the Kattegat, before turning south in the direction of ESRUM for a cross-section view of rural Zealand: winding lanes and beech forests, farmland cultivated to the road edge, traditional farmsteads with four wings surrounding a cobbled courtyard. At Esrum, follow the signs via JONSTRUP and drive along the Esrum Sø to the castle on the water's edge, **Fredensborg Slot.**

Built between 1719 and 1722, Fredensborg's a perfect example of Italian/Dutch baroque, on a small hill and surrounded by grounds which were the delight of King Frederik V, who turned this hunting seat into a royal summer residence. He held great parties here, and had statues erected in the leafy lakeside grounds, not to his peers but to ordinary people for a change, with exact renderings of folk costumes. You can stroll the grounds any time, but the royal apartments and private garden are opened to visitors only when the royal family is absent.

Nine kilometres more, to HILLERØD and you reach

Spiky sculptures at Louisiana Modern Art Museum contrast with
72 *traditional Danish countryside.*

Denmark's architectural showpiece, builder Christian IV's most monumental achievement, rightly described as one of the greatest Renaissance castles in northern Europe: **Frederiksborg Slot,** a brick and sandstone castle dramatically sited on three islands. During the years of the absolutist kings, all Danish monarchs were annointed and crowned there. In 1859 much of the interior was destroyed by fire, and it was left to Danish beer to rescue it nearly 20 years later.

Brewer J.C. Jacobsen's plan to restore the castle into a Danish Versailles—a museum of national history—was then approved by royal ordinance. Today, in more than 60 rooms, is a complete record of the Danish monarchy, from Christian I who established the Oldenburg line (1448–1863) through all subsequent monarchs of the next line, the Glücksburgs, down to the present queen.

Riddersalen (the Knights' Hall) and the chapel are Frederiksborg's ultimate triumph. The 185-foot Knights' Hall is awesome in its dimensions, with tapestried walls, marble floor and carved wooden ceiling, all reconstructed from old drawings after the 1859 fire.

74   Remarkably, below the

Knights' Hall, **Slotskirken** (the chapel) escaped virtually untouched in that infamous fire and remains a vision of gilt pillars and a high vaulted nave. Almost every inch is richly carved and ornamented. There are inset black marble panels with scriptural quotations, marquetry panels in ebony and rare

woods, and both altar and pulpit are in ebony with biblical scenes in silver relief. The **organ** is one of Europe's most notable, an almost unchanged original from 1610 by the Flemish master Esaias Compenius.

Around the gallery of this wondrous chapel—to many, one of the most abiding memories of a visit to Denmark—the window piers and recesses are hung with coats-of-arms of the knights of both the Order of the Elephant and the Order of the Grand Cross of

Frederiksborg Castle—Denmark's architectural showpiece with over 60 rooms of royalty on record.

Dannebrog. Look around you, and you'll spot some modern recipients, such as Sir Winston Churchill and Eisenhower.

A stroll around the cobbled courtyards, a rest by the 1620 **Neptune Fountain,** and it's onto the A5 back to Copenhagen, a 20-mile drive.

Frederiksborg Castle is open every day all year round: April: 11 a.m.–4 p.m. May–Sept.: 10 a.m.–5 p.m.; October: 10 a.m.–4 p.m.; Nov.–March: 11 a.m.–3 p.m. Without a car, it can be independently reached by regular S-train service to Hillerød. Sightseeing tours are available from Copenhagen most of the year round.

Roskilde

With its 800-year-old cathedral containing the splendid tombs of 37 monarchs, with Viking ships salvaged from its fjord and now presented in a unique maritime museum, with young scientists welcoming visitors to their prehistoric village nearby, Roskilde is a temptress beckoning tourists to make the brief (20–30-minute) journey from Copenhagen.

Whether you go by car, excursion bus or train, make

straight for the centre of this small, neat town and for the three green, needle-like spires which have been dominating the flat landscape for miles. This is **Domkirken** (the Cathedral) begun as a wooden church by King Harald Bluetooth around 1000 when he was converted to Christianity. Then, in the 1170s, Bishop Ab-

Royal tombs at Roskilde Cathedral —and a warm Iron Age welcome at Oldtidsbyen, the Ancient Village.

salon, founder of Copenhagen, started to build a brick and stone cathedral for his new bishopric, and over the next 300 years it grew into the Romanesque-Gothic amalgam of today. Christian IV, of course, couldn't be left out of the building scene, and in 1635 added the distinctive spires. He also built his own burial chapel and a gilded royal pew in the north wall of the church, heavily latticed and shielded from public view so that (it is said) he

could smoke his pipe in peace during Sunday services.

Nearly all Danish kings and queens since the first Margrete (d. 1412) are buried here.

The sarcophagi and chapels are all different, a jumbled symphony of style. The chapel of King Frederik V on the south side is a simple space of white paint and Norwegian marble, with 12 tombs grouped around it. In contrast, the Christian IV chapel on the north side is marked by amazingly elaborate 1618 wrought-ironwork and mainly 19th-century interior decoration.

A light note is introduced by the novel clock high on the south-west wall of the nave. But be there on the hour to see the 500-year-old wooden figures enact their timeless drama. As each hour arrives, St. George and his horse rear up, a dragon beneath them utters a shrill cry, a woman figure strikes her little bell four times with a hammer, the man his big bell once.

The chapel outside the cathedral by the northwestern tower was inaugurated in 1985 and dedicated in honour of Frederik IX, King of Denmark from 1947 to 1972, who is buried there.

To the front of the church is the traditional square, Stændertorvet, of this old market town, with outdoor café tables in good weather and replete with fruit, flower and vegetable stalls every Wednesday and Saturday morning. On Saturdays, also, there's a popular local flea market. To the rear is a sweep of public parkland, where you can walk down to the fjord and **Vikingeskibshallen** (the Viking Ship Museum).

When 11th-century Danes wanted to block the sea-route to Roskilde from ravaging Norwegians, they sank five Viking ships across a narrow neck of the shallow Roskilde fjord. It is these ships, excitingly salvaged in 1962, that form the basis of the Viking Ship Museum.

The museum building is on the edge of the water with one side completely glass to bring the fjord almost into the room. The shape of each ship has been reconstructed in metal strips, and the thousands of pieces of wood were placed in position after chemical conservation and drying out.

The museum is lavishly illustrated with photographs and charts, and free film shows are given in the cinema-cellar, telling the full story of the salvage in English.

All told, Roskilde is a go-ahead town with lively public entertainment—an open-air theatre and fjord boat trips in summer, concerts and cattle shows, bonfires and fireworks.

If you are going by train, ask at Copenhagen Station for the special Roskilde ticket *(Roskilde særtilbud)*, which covers the rail journey there and back, plus entrance to both cathedral and ship museum.

Ten kilometres south-west, by LEJRE, is the Historical-Archaeological Research Centre **Oldtidsbyen** (Ancient Town). Here, a group of enthusiasts are not only living in Iron-Age style, in clay and reed houses that look like a cluster of shaggy dogs, they are also conducting a major long-term scientific experiment, attempting to trace the effect on the environment of primitive man's use of tools—basically, how his needs and life-style destroyed and amended the natural amenities, how forest and wildlife disappeared, etc.

Every year, 80,000 visitors flock to Lejre to see the animal farm, the workshops, the explanatory film shows in Danish and English and, of course, to peep into the prehistoric houses with their smoky interiors and utterly primitive living conditions.

The village is open daily from 10 a.m. to 5 p.m. Apr. 30–Sept. 30; closed in winter.

What to Do

Shopping

Even husbands can enjoy shopping in Copenhagen. It's a quality experience, whether you're looking for fine furnishings or artistic clothes pegs.

Shopping Hours
Generally, all shops open at 9 a.m. and close at 5.30 p.m., Monday to Thursday. Late-night shopping extends to 7 or 8 p.m. on Fridays, and sometimes on Thursdays also. N.B.: Some shops (often food) are closed on Monday or Tuesday, and Saturday is early closing day at noon or 2 p.m.

On Sundays and national holidays, several shops open part-day, usually in the morning—bakers', florists', *smørrebrød* shops, sweet shops and kiosks.

Late-night shopping is possible every day till 10 p.m. or midnight at the Central Station which is like a cheery village with a 24-hour heel bar, Copenhagen's one remaining shoeshine, a supermarket, banks open for foreign exchange, a post office, room-booking service and snack bars. **79**

There are several central 24-hour shops (look for the sign *dag og nat shop*) with fresh bread from 3 a.m. and other food, beer and spirits.

Where to Shop

The linked pedestrians-only streets of Strøget/Fiolstræde/Købmagergade offer the total range: the finest ceramics and

silver shops, probably the best art-household store in the world, Copenhagen's leading furriers, antique shops by the score (also in the smaller streets branching off), young potters' and silversmiths' workshops, clothes and knitwear, toys and pipes, dozens of souvenir shops and kiosks.

Slightly off the beaten track, unless you're visiting Amalienborg and the Marble Church, is Bredgade/Store Kongensgade with a big range of boutiques.

What to Buy

Danish porcelain: The secret of its soft poetic effect is an underglaze technique shared only by Royal Copenhagen Porcelain (founded in 1775) and Bing & Grøndahl (1853) and allowing landscape pastels to be reproduced, and even accurate skin colours. Blue motifs come out particularly well. All pieces from these companies are hand-painted after a quick first firing, and then fired again for glazing at 2,600 °F. No two pieces are exactly alike. Anything from ashtrays to a 100-piece dinner service with a range of prices to match.

The market in unusual modern ceramics has been

Quality's the word for Copenhagen shopping—breathtaking displays of furniture and irresistible antiques. **81**

dominated for a good ten years by the stylized, humorous and highly decorative work of Bjørn Wiinblad. You'll see his spiky figures, plates, vases and ashtrays everywhere.

Silver is another Danish speciality, dominated by the name Georg Jensen. Silver in Denmark is quality-controlled and must be hallmarked. The Jensen showrooms offer creations ranging from key rings to precious jewellery.

Glassware and household products in **stainless steel** are particularly good buys if you want top design matched with excellent craftsmanship to take back home. There's still a thriving tradition of mouth-blown glass.

Furniture is among the world's best. Here you'll see items credited to the designer rather than the factory. Furniture is a national pride and nearly all good pieces will have a black circular "Danish Furniture-Makers' Control" sticker attached.

Lamps are again a lovingly designed product, as are **household textiles** and **hand-woven rugs.** In all these areas, the Danes' regard for home aesthetics shines through.

Furs are fantastic quality, if you can afford a Danish mink as well as the holiday.

Knitwear is Nordic-style, often highly patterned, warm and perhaps expensive.

Antiques are plentiful, especially of the home-spun rather than the fine-art variety; sniff around in the old town area.

Amber necklaces almost flow out of the Strøget shops and onto the pavement. The local "gem" (actually fossil resin) found in the southern Baltic, is probably cheaper here than back home.

Pipes are another indigenous craft. You pay for age of wood and quality of hand-crafted design. Hand-carved briars using 200-year-old wood will last 20–30 years.

Toys are simple and attractive, especially those in solid wood: trains, ships, etc. You'll also see hundreds of the Danish wooden soldier in all sizes.

Souvenirs are myriad: little mermaids, Copenhagen dolls in black lace caps and frilly skirts, ceramic blue figurines and animals and all kinds of trolls and Vikings abound, plus hand-painted spoons, racks and pepper-mills. An Amager shelf would make another memorable reminder. This is a group of three or four small hand-painted shelves in a triangular frame which hangs on the wall—beware of cheap versions.

Aquavit *(akvavit)* is the local tipple, the Danish *snaps*, usually flavoured with caraway seed—less expensive than imported spirits. It's cheapest at the airport's duty-free shop.

VAT, or sales tax, called MOMS in Denmark, is around 22 per cent on all products and services. This tax will be re-funded to visitors who make large purchases in shops displaying the red-and-white "Danish Tax-Free Shopping" sticker. Ask for details in the shop.

Skilled workmanship at the porcelain factory.

Relaxing

When in Copenhagen, relax ... as the Danes do. Hire a bike for a new view of life, stroll the beech woods and parks, have a night on the town at a concert or jazz club—or simply sit on one of the many public benches for a snack and a smoke. Here it's completely acceptable to consume your *smørrebrød* and green bottles of Danish lager as the world passes by. Ladies, take a cigar afterwards if you feel like it, nobody in Denmark will turn a hair.

Cycling: More than a sport, it's a way of life. Some hotels lend bicycles free to guests. Otherwise they're easy to hire (see p. 106). Ride the extensive network of cycle paths *(cykelsti)* with no worry from cars—or the weather: if it starts to rain, country buses will pack the bike on top. Taxis, too, have a special rack where your bike can accompany you back to the hotel for a small extra charge.

The beach: Bellevue Beach is only 20 minutes away by S-train (line C) to Klampenborg—so easy, you'll be part of a city exodus on sunny days.

Dyrehaven: Beside the rail station for Bellevue Beach is the entrance to the Royal Deer Park, now open to all and stretching for miles. Go by horse and carriage to see the deer feeding—but check carefully on prices.

Bakken amusement park is on the edge of the park not far from Bellevue. It's older than Tivoli and also more basic, with a big dipper and beer hall, circus revue and hall of distorting mirrors, bingo, porno and panto, a children's play park (look for *børnelegeplads*), fun-

Cycling: not so much a sport, more a way of life in Denmark. When you're tired, pack the bikes on a taxi—or even on top of your bus.

fairs and a wide choice of eating houses: take the opportunity of having *æbleskiver som vor mor bager dem*, "apple slices like mother makes" (deep-fried in batter). Very Danish.

Zoo: Copenhagen's Zoologisk Have is one of Europe's finest, and a veteran nearly 120 years old. More than 2,500 animals plus a good children's section, restaurant and cafeteria. Open all year from 9 a.m. to sunset or latest at 6 p.m.; Roskildevej 32, a 10-minute ride from Rådhuspladsen by buses 28 and 41.

Botanical gardens: Keen gardeners could spend two or three days here, examining the 70 laid-out areas, the palm house and various other greenhouses on this 25-acre Botanisk Have site opposite Rosenborg Castle. Open year-round till sunset. Get there by bus No. 14 from Rådhuspladsen, Nos. 7 and 17 from Kongens Nytorv.

Circus: Almost opposite Tivoli, down Axeltorv. Established in 1887 and voted Continental Europe's best circus for four consecutive years. Shows every night, May to October, with concerts, musicals and ballets the rest of the year.

Industrial Art Tours: Visit a porcelain or silver factory with an organized bus tour (see p. 122) to learn how these exquisite items reach the shops.

Breweries: Try a brewery tour, not only to sample a free bottle or two, but also to discover how every glass you drink is a positive contribution to art, science or industry: both Carlsberg and Tuborg donate vast sums through their charitable foundations. Carlsberg (also with a museum) welcomes you at the Elephant Gate, Ny Carlsbergvej 140 (bus No. 6 from Rådhuspladsen) for guided tours in several languages at 9 a.m., 11 a.m. and 2.30 p.m. You can visit Tuborg (Strandvej 54; bus No. 1 from Rådhuspladsen) from 8.30 a.m. to 2.30 p.m. Both breweries Monday to Friday only.

Music, Opera: Scores of concerts year-round at the Royal Theatre, Tivoli, the Royal Conservatory of Music, Radio House, in churches and museums. The Danish Radio Symphony Orchestra and the Royal Danish Opera are only just below world top.

Ballet: The Royal Danish Ballet is world-famed, and rightly so; one of Europe's oldest, with a 200-year-old repertory. The company experiments in modern dance too (even nude rock ballet), but its great tradition is Bournonville classics which you should see.

The Ballet performs from September to June only.

Jazz: Copenhagen is now claimed to be Europe's leading jazz centre. Some of the main clubs/bars offer jazz of all sorts every night till 2 or later. Many foreign stars now live in Denmark and appear at leading clubs, like Club Mont-

Tivoli pantomime: mid-summer entertainment for young and old.

martre in Nørregade. There's free jazz at smaller bars.

Folk, Rock: Four folk venues in the downtown area near the University. One rock dance- **87**

hall. Free rock concerts on summer Sundays in Fælled Park.

Cinemas: Films are shown in their original language with Danish sub-titles.

Nightclubs: Take advice from your hotel receptionist if you want to avoid (or find) clubs that specialize in girls rather than floor-shows. Some first-class specimens of both kinds.

Discos: Routine is to enrol as a member at the door. They range from downbeat discotheques to sophisticated hotel nightclubs.

Sex clubs/cinemas: Formerly disfiguring Strøget and generally offending visitors, Copenhagen's notorious sex emporia have mostly moved to the less conspicuous Istedgade/Halmtorvet area west of Central Station. Not much is left, though—only some cheap "nightclubs" and second-rate pornographic cinemas.

Café life: A different fare altogether. Relaxed, welcom-

ing. Sit as long as you like over a beer or coffee—look at the often eccentric décor and meet the Danes simultaneously. Especially friendly bars around the University.

At home: If invited to a Danish home, grab the chance. Note the attention paid to cosy and often elegant living. Gear yourself down to leisurely eating and drinking, but don't *skål* the hostess too frequently, as she likes to keep her head while entertaining.

Festivals

Denmark has no great religious festivals and processions, no spectacular state ceremonies such as coronations. But "festivities" are in the air all the time, and you only have to look at *Copenhagen This Week* to see the quantity of events going on.

One or two specials, however:

Viking Festival—*Vikingespil* (mid-June to early July). The annual junket of plays, mead and barbecues at Frederikssund (many bus tours available).

St. John's Eve—*Sankt Hansaften* (June 23). Bonfires lit all along the "Riviera" coastline north of Copenhagen to drive the witches away on their broomsticks to Blocksberg in Germany.

Copenhagen Summer Festival, involving pop concerts, chamber music, takes place in different parts of the city, with admission free. Look in the *Copenhagen This Week* for details.

Roskilde Festival (late June to early July). Greatest pop festival in Northern Europe, with jazz and rock in a delightful setting.

Folk-dancers in alfresco frolics. **89**

Sports

There's plenty for all within easy reach of Copenhagen. Top spectator sport is football (soccer). Top participator sports are sailing and fishing. Danish tourist offices keep up-to-date lists of all facilities, telephone numbers, etc. Remember in Copenhagen the excellent information office at H.C. Andersens Boulevard 22.

Archery: In the suburban Valby Idrætspark, May–October.

Bowling: Three alleys in town, two of them closed in July.

Cycle racing: Very popular, and an experience worth catching up with. Normally Mondays or Tuesdays, May–September, at Ordrup cycle track *(cykelbane)*. Take the S-train to Charlottenlund.

Fishing: Jutland is the Danish mecca for sea fishing, but you can still go for Øresund cod, mackerel, flat-fish and gar-pike from Amager and the coast north of town. No special permit is required for fishing in Denmark, either in lakes or river—a real boost to anglers. You can hire licensed boats on Lyngby, Bagsværd and Furesø lakes on the north-west edge of town.

Flying: Private planes, gliders and models available through the Royal Danish Aero Club *(Kongelig Dansk Aeroklub)* at Copenhagen Airport.

Golf: More than 30 clubs in Denmark, eight within 25 miles of Copenhagen, the nearest in Klampenborg suburb at Dyrehaven 2, tel. 31630483. Green fees throughout Denmark are moderate, and foreigners are welcomed.

Horse-racing: Also at Klampenborg, the track *(galopbane)* is open mainly Saturdays from mid-April to mid-December. S-train to Klampenborg and bus 160.

Riding: Good riding, particularly in the Deer Park. Several stables and schools in the area—look in the *Fagbog* (telephone directory to trade and professions) under *Rideundervisning.*

Rowing: A major sporting activity, with an Olympic course and many clubs. Information from the Danish Rowing Association *(Dansk Forening for Rosport),* Vester Voldgade 91, 1552 Copenhagen V.

Sailing: Join the Sound and

Beach dress is optional, topless is commonplace. A Danish day out means relaxation as you please.

inland lake throngs. Yachts and cruisers available for hire. Evidence of navigational proficiency required for Øresund sailing, where close watch must be kept for the constant ferry traffic. Book in advance with help from your local Danish tourist office (see p. 124).

Skating: Many stretches of water within the city boundaries freeze up in winter. Alternatively, there's an indoor skating rink *(skøjtehal)* at Copenhagen Forum and at other suburban locations. All open October–April.

Soccer: Largely amateur, but of high standard. Every weekend from April to June and August to November, and some weekday afternoons in May, June and September. Main Copenhagen stadium at Idrætsparken.

Swimming: Sea bathing all along the Zealand coast to the north and south of the city, but the water is rarely warm. Nude bathing mainly at Tisvildeleje,

away round the north coast, but practised elsewhere, *provided* other bathers aren't offended. Approximately a dozen indoor swimming baths, some with sauna/massage and gymnasium facilities.

Tennis: Guest membership of local clubs available for a small fee, and foreign players made welcome. Tourist office has all addresses.

Trotting: Spectator sport second only to football, at the Charlottenlund course en route to Klampenborg.

Water-skiing: A popular sport on the Furesø. Consult tourist offices for latest information.

The social scene at Klampenborg racetrack. Meanwhile the winner...

Wining and Dining

Food is not—quite—an obsession, but it's taken seriously and the standard is high. Though a Dane at home will not normally devour those gargantuan breakfasts offered to tourists in their hotels, he'll happily spend two hours over his *frokost* (lunch) *smørrebrød,* or up to four if he's entertaining special guests, and a dinner *(middag)* in celebratory mood can last from 6 p.m. to . . . infinity.*

Restaurants and Bars

There are more than 2,000 restaurants, cafés, bars and snack-bars in Copenhagen. Restaurants often serve a special dish of the day *(dagens ret)* and the "Dan-menu"—a two-course Danish lunch or dinner at a fixed price—in addition to *à la carte* items. Look out for a *daglig kort* ("daily card") which usually features less expensive dishes than those listed on the more formal menu *(spisekort).* You'll also find little lunch-only, cosy cellar restaurants, listed in *Copenhagen This Week*—good value, "old-world" charm and much frequented by Danes themselves. Out of town, a *kro* (country inn) can provide a charming if sometimes expensive décor for a special meal.

For a drink in the evening (or in fact practically any time of day or night, since opening hours are very liberal), drop into one of the numerous cafés, pubs or bars dotted throughout the city. A more traditionally Danish type of drinking establishment is the *værtshus,* which may be tidy or tatty, depending on the neighbourhood.

Value-added tax and service charge are automatically added to your bill. Danes are not tip-minded, though after a meal out you may want to round off the bill.

Breakfast

Breakfast *(morgenmad)* in a Danish hotel is a far cry from the Spartan "continental breakfast" of a bread roll and a cup of coffee. Bread rolls, meat, cheese, jam, pastries and possibly an egg are accompanied by a glass of milk or fruit juice followed by tea or coffee.

Cold Food

Cold food is Denmark's outstanding culinary speciality. You'll soon learn to indulge

---

* The Berlitz DANISH FOR TRAVELLERS phrase-book, the DANISH-ENGLISH, ENGLISH-DANISH pocket dictionary and the 14-language EUROPEAN MENU READER all include extensive glossaries of Danish food with English equivalents.

prodigiously in this national tradition.

Smørrebrød are essentially thickly buttered slices of rye or white bread covered with one of a variety of delicacies: veal *(kalvekød)*, beef tartare *(bøf tartar)*, liver paste *(leverpostej)*, salmon *(laks)*, smoked eel *(røget ål)*, cod-roe *(torskerogn)*, shrimps *(rejer)*, herring *(sild)*, ham *(skinke)*, roast beef *(roast beef)*, salad *(salat)* or cheese *(ost)*. This main layer is garnished with a variety of accessories carefully selected to enhance both taste and appearance. Larger restaurants have scores of different *smørrebrød*. You usually tick off your orders on the menu itself, specifying your choice of bread (*rugbrød:* rye; *franskbrød:* white; *pumpernikkel:* black bread; *knækbrød:* crispbread). Two or three of these substantial "open sandwiches" will generally satisfy most appetites. But just to give you an idea, one Copenhagen restaurant offers 178 varieties of *smørrebrød*.

Don't confuse *smørrebrød* with the Swedish word *smörgåsbord* which has acquired international currency to describe the pan-Scandinavian cold buffet-style spread, known in Denmark as the *koldt bord* ("cold table"). Especially larger restaurants offer an eye-boggling array of dishes in their *koldt bord.* For a fixed price, you start at one end of the table helping yourself to herring in various preparations, seafood, mayonnaise salads and other delicacies, and continue on to sample liver paste, ham and other cuts of meat. Despite its name, a *koldt bord* always includes a few hot items, such as meat balls, pork sausages, soup and fried potatoes. Several kinds of bread and salads are also provided.

En platte is a cold dish (smaller version of previous) made up of six to eight specialities, often eaten at lunchtime.

Aquavit (see p. 83) and beer go especially well with a *koldt bord.*

Fish

Fish (or small canapés) is the traditional first course of a full-course meal. It is also available individually, of course. And fish is on the Danish menu in great variety. Herring is a great favourite, served pickled, marinated or fried, with a sherry, vinegar, curry or fennel dressing. The succulent red Greenland shrimps are keen competitors in the popularity stakes. Lobster is widely available (but not cheap), as is crab, salmon, cod and halibut. **95**

The little Øresund *rødspætte* (red-spot plaice) is on every menu. A speciality in summer is *danske rejer*, the small pink shrimps from local waters, served piled high on white bread.

Predictably, Copenhagen's three best fish restaurants are to be found in the Gammel Strand area.

Meat

Until a few years ago, Danish meat dishes consisted almost entirely of pork and veal. Lamb is now appearing on menus and beef has made a major breakthrough as Danish farmers breed more cattle for slaughter. The commonest steaks are *fransk bøf*, filet steak

served with herb butter and chips (French fries), and *engelsk bøf,* filet steak served with fried onions and potatoes.

Top restaurants cook in classic French style. In small establishments, however, some typical Danish hot dishes remain; *mørbradbøf* is a delectable legacy of the pork-only days: small steaks of what is called tenderloin in English, lean, very tasty and served as a main course with onions, gravy and boiled potatoes.

Smørrebrød *and beer—Danish contributions to good living…*

For more ordinary fare, tasty nevertheless, what about Danish meatballs *(frikadeller)*, a finely minced mixture of pork and veal, often served with potato salad. *Biksemad* is cheap and tasty: a Danish hash of diced potatoes, onions and meat with a fried egg on top. *Hakkebøf* is the crumbling Danish hamburger—and *pariserbøf* is a slightly cooked, almost raw, hamburger topped with raw egg yolk, raw onion, capers, horse-radish, etc.

Salads

The word for salad, *salat*, has two meanings. It can be the usual side-dish of fresh lettuce, sliced egg, tomato and plentiful red peppers; or, more often, it's one of several mayonnaise mixtures often eaten on *smørrebrød* or as an appetizer. *Italiensk salat* consists of diced carrots, asparagus, peas and macaroni. *Skinkesalat* is basically chopped ham, and *sildesalat* comprises marinated or pickled herring, beetroot, apple and pickles. These are only some of the most common of the many sandwich salads available.

Cheese and Fruit

Danish Blue *(Danablu)*—rich, with a sharp flavour—is quite well known internationally.

Mycella—similar but milder—is found rarely outside the country. *Fynbo* and *Samsø* are both mild, firm cheeses with a sweetish nutty flavour. In addition, Denmark produces honest imitations of French, Swiss and Dutch cheeses.

Fruit follows cheese if you're eating out, and if Denmark's northerly latitude means her fruit is largely imported, the country is nevertheless rich in various kinds of berries.

Desserts

It will have been obvious from the very start that Denmark is not for dieting. And by the time you get your Danish desserts your best intentions will have been quite definitely routed! Your dessert will be lavishly laced with cream *(fløde)* or whipped cream *(flødeskum)*.

Favourite desserts include: *æblekage* (stewed apples with vanilla, served with alternating layers of biscuit crumbs—and topped with whipped cream) and *bondepige med slør* (a mixture of rye-bread crumbs, apple sauce, sugar—and whipped cream).

Snacks

For a snack with a difference, try deep-fried Camembert cheese served with toast and strawberry jam *(ristet fransk-*

brød med friturestegt camembert og jordbærsyltetøj).

The university area is good for economical goulashes, hashes and chicken and *håndmadder* (usually three thin *smørrebrød* with different toppings). The ubiquitous hotdog stands *(pølsevogn)* serve red Danish sausages *(pølse)* with mustards and relishes.

Oddly enough, Danish pastry is called Viennese pastry *(wienerbrød)* in Denmark. This distinctive light and flaky delight can be found in any *konditori,* and, with the calories battle abandoned, makes a scrumptious mid-morning or afternoon snack.

Drinks

The golden Danish lager comes in several types, from *lys pilsner* (light lager) at only 2 per cent alcohol, through the normal green-bottle *pilsner* to the stouts and special beers (like *elefantøl*) at 6–7 per cent or more. *Pilsner* is available everywhere almost 24 hours a day. In cafés it costs three or four times the shop price. The rarer draught beer *(fadøl)* is less carbonated and slightly cheaper.

Akvavit is the fiery Danish *snaps*, made from potatoes, often with a distinct caraway taste, taken at mealtimes with the opening fish course, and often later with the cheese. Beware of over-indulging, or you'll need *Gammel Dansk* bitter for next morning's hangover. If you order *akvavit* with your meal, the bottle may well be put on the table for you to help yourself. Don't be deluded into thinking you'll be charged for only one measure: back in the bar they'll know exactly how much has disappeared.

All wine is imported and expensive in restaurants. Even cheap house-wine *(husets vin)* can cost three times the supermarket price.

After dinner you might like a glass of Denmark's famous cherry liqueur, *Cherry Heering*.

Non-Alcoholic Beverages

An increasingly popular non-alcoholic beer has been introduced which looks and tastes exactly like *pilsner* and costs the same.

Coffee *(kaffe)* is everywhere good and strong and served with real cream. The basic charge may seem high, but the waiter will usually come round offering refills.

On a chilly day you might like to try *varm kakao med flødeskum*—hot cocoa with whipped cream.

Skål! . . . and tak!
Learn to say *skål* (the vowel is somewhere between *loll* and *hall*) with your beer or *akvavit*. It's more than just Danish for "cheers"—it's a ritual if you are invited to a Danish home for dinner. Your host usually has privilege of first toast. He will raise his glass, pointing it towards everyone in turn, looking directly at them—and say *skål*. After everyone has taken a sip, or a substantial swallow, he will look at them all again in turn, still with the glass raised, before putting it back on the table.

And after the meal, the appropriate—and essential—formula is *tak for mad* (pronounced *tak for maad*), which means, simply, "thanks for the meal".

To Help You Order...

Could we have a table?
Do you have a set menu?

Må vi få et bord?
Har De en dagens ret?

I'd like a/an/some...

Jeg vil gerne have...

beer	**en øl**	napkin	**en serviet**
bread	**brød**	pepper	**peber**
coffee	**kaffe**	potatoes	**kartofler**
dessert	**en dessert**	salad	**en salat**
fish	**fisk**	salt	**salt**
glass	**et glas**	soup	**suppe**
ice-cream	**is**	sugar	**sukker**
meat	**kød**	tea	**te**
menu	**et spisekort**	vegetables	**grønsager**
milk	**mælk**	(iced) water	**(is)vand**
mustard	**sennep**	wine	**vin**

...and Read the Menu

agurkesalat	cucumber salad	**lever**	liver
blomkål	cauliflower	**løg**	onion
citron	lemon	**medisterpølse**	pork sausage
flæskesteg	roast pork with crackling	**mørbradbøf**	fried fillet of pork
frikadelle	fried meat ball	**nyrer**	kidney
grøn peber	green pepper	**oksekød**	beef
grønne bønner	french beans	**ost**	cheese
gulerødder	carrots	**porre**	leek
hamburgerryg	loin of pork	**pommes frites**	chips (french fries)
hindbær	raspberries	**rejer**	shrimps
jordbær	strawberries	**rødkål**	red cabbage
kalvekød	veal	**sild**	herring
kartoffelmos	mashed potatoes	**skinke**	ham
kirsebær	cherries	**svinekød**	pork
kotelet	chop	**søtunge**	sole
kylling	chicken	**æble**	apple
kål	cabbage	**æg**	egg
lagkage	layer cake	**æggekage**	omelet
laks	salmon	**ørred**	trout
		ål	eel

101

BLUEPRINT for a Perfect Trip

How to Get There

If the choice of ways to go is bewildering, the complexity of fares and regulations can be downright stupefying. A reliable travel agent will have full details of all the latest flight possibilities, fares and regulations.

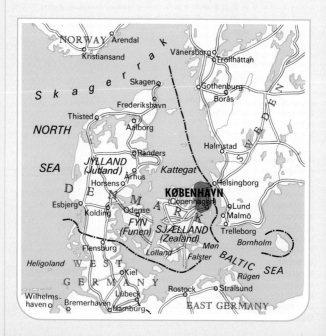

BY AIR

Copenhagen Airport (see also p. 105) is on several intercontinental routes—mainly from North America and the Middle and Far East. There are frequent regional services from most European cities. Average journey time London–Copenhagen is 1 hour and 45 minutes, New York–Copenhagen 7 hours and 40 minutes.

BY RAIL/SEA/CAR

Ferry services to Denmark are generally into Esbjerg (from the U.K.), to Gedser (from Germany) and to numerous ports (including Copenhagen itself) for travellers arriving from Norway and Sweden.

The *Nordic Tourist Ticket* permits 21 days of unlimited rail travel in Denmark, Finland, Norway and Sweden. *Inter-Rail cards* and *Eurailpasses* are also valid in Denmark.

There are road and rail links into Jutland from Schleswig-Holstein in Germany, and through-trains from Hamburg to Copenhagen.

When to Go

Denmark's relatively temperate climate is due to its situation and the sea currents, but its changeable weather is caused by frequent switches in the wind's direction. Spring comes late perhaps, but summer is often sunny and autumn mild.

Approximate monthly temperature, Copenhagen:

	J	F	M	A	M	J	J	A	S	O	N	D
°C	0.5	0	2	6	11	16	17	16	13	9	5	2
°F	33	32	35	42	52	60	63	61	56	48	40	36

Planning Your Budget

The following are some average prices in Danish kroner for basic expenses. However, remember that all prices must be regarded as *approximate*.

Airport transfer. Bus to Rådhuspladsen 12 kr. Special airport bus directly to Central Station 24 kr., taxi 100 kr. (tip included).

Baby-sitters. 25 kr. per hour. Booking fee 25 kr., plus transport.

Bicycle hire. 30 kr. a day, 140 kr. a week, deposit 100 kr.

Camping. Camping pass for foreign visitors 48 kr. per family, 25 kr. per person per night, children half price.

Car hire. *Ford Escort 1.3* 310 kr. per day, 2 kr. per kilometre (over 100 km.), 2,030 kr. per week with max. 700 km. *VW Minibus* (9 seats) 675 kr. per day, 3 kr. per km., 3,780 kr. per week with max. 700 km.

Cigarettes. Approx. 26 kr. per packet of 20.

Copenhagen card. One day 90 kr., two days 140 kr., three days 180 kr. Half price for children between 5 and 11.

Entertainment. Cinema 50 kr., Royal Ballet tickets 120 kr., nightclub entry 20–50 kr. Tivoli: adults 27 kr., children 13 kr.

Hairdressers. *Woman's* haircut 250 kr., shampoo and set 180 kr., permanent wave 380 kr., dye/tint 220 kr. *Man's* haircut 180 kr.

Hotels. Top class 1,800 kr., medium 900 kr., moderate 400 kr. for double room.

Meals and drinks (at a fairly good establishment). Lunch 90 kr., dinner 150 kr., sandwich *(smørrebrød)* 25 kr., coffee 10 kr., aquavit *(snaps)* 25 kr., beer 15 kr., soft drink 11 kr.

Public transport. Flat-rate ticket *(grundbillet)* for single bus or S-train ride 8 kr. Ticket coupons *(rabatkort)* for 10 rides: yellow 70 kr., green 125 kr., grey 190 kr.

Shopping bag. Bread 7 kr., 250 g. of butter 10 kr., 6 eggs 9 kr., ½ kg. of beefsteak (choice meat) 40 kr., ½ kg. of coffee 25 kr., 250 g. of instant coffee 15 kr., bottle of beer 6 kr., soft drink 4 kr.

Taxi. Meter charge around 12 kr.; plus about 7 kr. per km. (tip incl.) in the daytime, plus 9.30 kr. per km. (tip incl.) evenings and weekends.

An A–Z Summary of Practical Information and Facts

Listed after some main entries is an appropriate Danish translation, usually in the singular. You'll find this vocabulary useful when asking for information or assistance.

For all prices, refer to list on p. 104.

ACCOMMODATION—see **HOTELS**

A

AIRPORT *(lufthavn)*. Copenhagen Airport, around 10 kilometres from the city centre, is one of Europe's busiest. It's also a major gateway to Europe for overseas travellers from the U.S.A., Canada, Japan, Australia and many other countries in the Far East and Africa. Something like 40 airlines have regular flights to and from Copenhagen. Danish domestic flights also link up with destinations in Jutland, as well as with Funen and Bornholm islands, and various domestic flight concessions are made for foreign visitors.

Buses run directly from the airport to the main railway station in central Copenhagen, 30 minutes away. Others go to the port of Dragør (south of the airport) for the ferry connection to Limhamn in southern Sweden; yet a third bus service leaves for the downtown hydrofoil crossing to Malmö.

Both porters and luggage trolleys are available. Taxis abound (for fare, see p. 104).

Copenhagen Airport provides a good shopping centre, with duty-free self-service stores and a variety of boutiques and gift and souvenir shops, including souvenirs from Greenland. There's a bank, post office, nursery, a barber's shop and ladies' hairdresser, shower rooms, rest centre, Danish food shops, restaurant and a large snack-bar area—last chance for a *smørrebrød* and *wienerbrød* feast.

Where's the bus for...?   **Hvorfra afgår bussen til...?**

B **BABY-SITTERS.** Hotel receptionists or the nearest tourist office are likely to know of some local baby-sitting service; otherwise, consult telephone listings under *Babysitters* in the directory to trade and professions *(Fagbog).*

Can you get me a baby-sitter for tonight?	**Kan De skaffe mig en babysitter til i aften?**

BANKS and CURRENCY-EXCHANGE OFFICES *(bank; vekselkontor).* Copenhagen's banks are open from 9.30 a.m. to 4 p.m., Monday to Friday, except on Thursdays when they stay open till 6 p.m. In the provinces, hours fluctuate from town to town. Outside banking hours, exchange bureaux operate at the Central Station every day of the week from 7 a.m. to 9 p.m. and at the entrance to Tivoli in H.C. Andersens Boulevard from noon to 11 p.m. during the pleasure park's high season (May 1 to mid-September). Most large hotels will change foreign currency, but you'll get a better rate in banks, exchange bureaux and tourist offices. See also CREDIT CARDS.

BARBERS'—see **HAIRDRESSERS'**

BICYCLE HIRE *(cykeludlejning).* Why not join the Danes in a national pastime—touring country lanes and woodlands by bike? Tourist offices will refer you to local dealers, or, in Copenhagen, go to the "Københavns Cykelbørs" cycle-hire depot at Nørre Farimagsgade 69 (tel.: 33 14 07 17). From April to October cycles can also be hired at many railway stations—nearest to Copenhagen are Klampenborg, Lyngby, Hillerød and Helsingør—but advance booking is necessary, so call Central Station 33 14 17 01. On payment of a nominal freight charge, if you prefer, return the bike to another railway station in the country. Organized cycling tours can be arranged through tourist offices in your country or tour operators in Denmark. Routes cover about 25 to 30 miles a day, and you can choose to stay in a youth hostel, *kro* (inn) or hotel. It's all set out in the *Cycling Holidays in Denmark* leaflet obtainable free from the Danish Cyclist Federation and the Danish Tourist Board. Evidence of identity is always needed when hiring cycles. (N.B. bicycles travel free as "personal luggage" if you prefer to bring your own from home.)

CAMPING *(camping)*. More than 500 camping sites, eight of them less than 10 miles from the centre of Copenhagen, have received the seal of approval from the Camping Council, which means they are frequently visited by health and camping inspectors. The sites range frome one- to three-star categories and cover basics from drinking water to provision stores and the services of camp wardens. Unless you have an International Camping Carnet you obtain a Camping Pass for foreigners, valid for the rest of the year, at the first site visited. Camping on private land requires the owner's permission.

Buy the book listing all sites from Campingrådet, Olof Palmes gade 10, 2100 Copenhagen Ø (tel.: 31 42 32 22)—or pick up an excellent free brochure on camping, youth hostels and student hotels from the Danish Tourist Board in your country (see TOURIST INFORMATION OFFICES).

Note that maximum speed for cars towing caravans (trailers) in Denmark is 70 k.p.h. (kilometres per hour).

CANAL TOURS *(kanaltur)*. Though the city hasn't as extensive a network of canals as Venice or Amsterdam, Copenhagen's canals provide a delightful hour's trip on a fine day. Gammel Strand and Nyhavn (at Kongens Nytorv) are the two main starting points. From May to October, tours—some of them with a guided commentary—give you an excellent view of the inner city and harbour.

CAR FERRIES. Since Denmark is largely an archipelago, it's hardly surprising that car ferries are a familiar feature of the country's everyday life. Though spectacular bridges have been built linking some of the islands, a good many places can still only be reached by boat. You certainly won't be disappointed in the regular, efficient ferry services that conveniently cover the islands and the Jutland peninsula. All the major routes carry both cars and passengers. Detailed timetables including rates and conditions are available from the Danish National Tourist Board, in English. Fares vary according to the weight and length of the car; prices quoted may include passengers, so check beforehand. It's highly advisable to book a day ahead, at least for domestic crossings—the Danes do, especially in summer when boats tend to be quite full. Be in good time (30 minutes) for embarkation, otherwise you'll probably lose your reservation.

CAR HIRE *(biludlejning)*. There are several car hire counters at Copenhagen Airport, and the major international agencies are represented in the capital. Tourist information bureaux have lists of local **107**

C firms. Otherwise, look up under *Autoudlejning* in the trade telephone directory *(Fagbog)*.

To hire a car, you'll need to produce a valid national (or international) driving licence and be at least 20 years of age (25 for some firms). It's a good idea to have your passport available, too, although don't leave it with the company. Most agencies will require a cash deposit covering the estimated rental charge. Credit cards are accepted. Our "Planning Your Budget" section on page 104 gives you the standard rates of the major car-hire firms.

CIGARETTES, CIGARS, TOBACCO *(cigaretter, cigarer, tobak)*. Most international cigarette brands are readily available as well as good local ones, but prices are stiff, not to say prohibitive (see p. 104). A packet bought in bars or restaurants costs extra, the difference being… that the waiter will take off the plastic wrapping and open the packet for you.

Danes are discerning cigar and pipe smokers, and you'll find many comparatively cheap local brands as well as imported ones.

A packet of…/A box of matches, please.	**En pakke…/En æske tændstikker, tak.**
filter-tipped/without filter	**med/uden filter**

CLIMATE and CLOTHING. See also the "When to Go" section on page 103. Casual clothes will fit nearly every occasion, including theatre and most dining-out. Only in top-class hotels and clubs will men be required to wear a tie in the evening, and in these situations ladies will not look out of place in a formal dress. But for the rest it's go as you like.

Summer nights are long and light but often chilly, so a sweater or wrap is essential. Bring a light overcoat or raincoat too, in addition to ordinary summer clothes—the weather has an awkward habit of changing. On the beach, you can be as brief as you like (topless for younger women is almost the norm).

Spring and autumn have many hours of sunshine, but winter can be downright cold and you should pack plenty of warm clothes (plus a raincoat). In all seasons, comfortable walking shoes are much to be recommended for your tours around the cobbled old-town area.

CONSULATES—see EMBASSIES

CONVERTER CHARTS. For fluid and distance measures, see page 112. Denmark uses the metric system.

Temperature

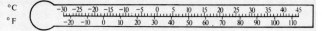

Length

Weight

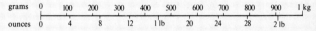

COPENHAGEN CARD. Similar to a plastic credit card, this discount tourist card offers unlimited travel on buses and trains in metropolitan Copenhagen, free entrance to many museums and sights and up to 50 per cent discount on ferry routes connecting Sealand with Sweden and on hydrofoils between Copenhagen and Malmö. The card is valid for one, two or three days and is on sale at travel agencies, and main railway stations in Denmark, and at certain Copenhagen hotels.

CREDIT CARDS and TRAVELLER'S CHEQUES *(kreditkort; rejse-check)*. Major hotels and many restaurants—and some tourist shops, too—will accept payment by international credit cards. There's little problem with traveller's cheques, either, if you have passport identification.

CRIME and THEFT. If Copenhagen generally still counts among the (relatively) safest capital cities to walk around in, things are not all they used to be. Pickpockets are rampant, and petty crime is on the increase. Take normal precautions. Keep a close eye on your belongings. Definitely hesitate before walking out alone in the wee hours through seedy areas—your hotel receptionist can give advice if in doubt about night-time locations you wish to visit. Avoid the Christiania area day and night.

C **CURRENCY.** The unit of Danish currency is the *krone*, abbreviated *kr.*, or, abroad, *Dkr.* (to distinguish it from the Norwegian and Swedish krone). It is divided into 100 *øre*.

Coins: 25 and 50 øre; 1, 5, 10 and 20 kroner.
Banknotes: 20, 50, 100, 500 and 1,000 kroner.

CUSTOMS CONTROLS *(toldkontrol).* See also ENTRY FORMALITIES and DRIVING IN DENMARK. The following chart shows customs allowances for items of personal use.

	Cigarettes		Cigars		Tobacco	Spirits		Dinner wine
1)	400	or	100	or	500 g.	1 l.	and	2 l.
2)	300	or	75	or	400 g.	1.5 l.	and	4 l.
3)	200	or	50	or	250 g.	1 l.	and	2 l.

1) residents outside Europe (1.5 l. of spirits and 4 l. wine if bought inside the EEC *not* tax free)
2) residents of Europe, non-tax-free goods bought in an EEC country
3) residents of Europe, tax-free-goods bought in an EEC country or goods obtained outside the EEC

Currency restrictions. There is no limit on the amount of Danish or foreign currency that can be brought into or taken out of the country by non-residents. However, anything over kr. 50,000 can be exported only if it does not exceed the amount originally imported.

D **DRIVING IN DENMARK.** To take your car into Denmark, you'll need:

● a valid driving licence, showing which type of vehicle it applies to
● car registration papers
● Green Card (an extension of your regular insurance policy, valid for travel abroad). Though not obligatory for EEC countries, it's still preferable to have it.
● a red warning triangle in case of breakdown
● a national identity sticker for your car

Driving conditions: Drive on the right, pass on the left. Traditionally, traffic coming from your right has priority, but this is decreasingly relevant in Denmark, where most junctions are clearly marked with white broken triangles (called "sharks' teeth" in Danish), halt signs, traffic lights, etc. Danish national policy is to abolish roundabouts, now considered dangerous because of priority confusion.

The Danes are, on the whole, well disciplined drivers and they will rightly expect you to be the same. Clear indication should always be given when changing lanes, either on motorways (expressways) or on the broad thoroughfares that cut through central Copenhagen. Weaving from one lane to another is a punishable offence.

Pedestrian crossings are sacrosanct and nearly always controlled by lights. When turning at lights, you *must* allow pedestrians on the road you are going to cross first; equally bikes have priority at any crossing if they want to go straight on when the car turns right.

Beware of buses pulling out from stops—you should give way to them. Caution, also, for cyclists and moped riders to your right, often on their own raised pathways *(cykelsti)*, but sometimes divided from you merely by a white line, which you should not cross.

Seat belts must be worn by both driver and passengers. Motor-cycle, moped and scooter drivers, and their passengers, must wear crash helmets. British car-owners note: left dipping headlights are illegal.

Speed limits: On the *motorvej* (motorway/expressway), the limit is 100 k.p.h. (kilometres per hour), i.e. 62 m.p.h. Other roads call for 80 k.p.h. (50 m.p.h.) and in built-up areas—indicated by white signs with town silhouettes—the speed limit drops to 50 k.p.h. (31 m.p.h.). Cars towing caravans (trailers) may not exceed 70 k.p.h. (44 m.p.h.). If caught speeding, you're in for a heavy fine—on the spot.

Parking: Traffic wardens in grey uniforms (and police) are active looking for motorists who have parked near signs reading *stopforbud* (no stopping) or *parkering forbudt* (no parking). They may only put a warning card on your windscreen, but they just might leave a ticket that'll mean a hefty fine. A car that causes a serious obstruction or is double-parked may well be towed away and impounded—and you'll have to pay for the towing, plus a fine. To judge whether you have parked longer than allowed where waiting is limited, the warden will look at the disc you should display on your windscreen, indicating the time you arrived. These discs (*P-skive* or *parkeringsskive)* can be obtained free from police stations, garages, post offices and most banks.

Stopping and waiting is not allowed within 5 metres of crossroads, pedestrian crossings or exits from cycle tracks. *Datostop* and *Dato-* **111**

D *parkering* mean that stopping or parking are allowed only on one side of the street—even numbers on even days, odd numbers on odd days. For parking meters you'll need 1-, 5- and 10-krone coins. Parked cars should by law be left locked.

Drinking and driving: With more than 0.8 millilitres of alcohol in your blood, you face a fine equivalent to a month's wages, lose your licence for a year and can be sent to a "lenient prison". No joking here.

Breakdown: If you have a breakdown, you can call FALCK, the breakdown and towing service, in Copenhagen at 33 14 22 22 day and night. Road assistance (only) is given free of charge to members of FIA or AIT motoring organizations. If you aren't a member, you should take out an insurance in your home country. Note that a MOMS (value-added tax) of 22 per cent is added to all repair bills.

Fuel and oil *(benzin; olie):* Service stations are plentiful, and most international brands of fuel are available, but expensive. However, you can save a few øre per litre at a self-service station (variously called *selvbetjening, tank selv* or "self-service").

Fluid measures

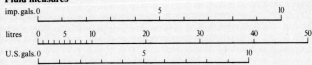

Distance

Road signs: International pictographs are in widespread use, but here are some written signs you may encounter:

Blind vej	Dead end road (cul-de-sac)
Fare	Danger
Fodgængere	Pedestrians
Indkørsel forbudt	No entry
Omkørsel	Diversion
Rabatten er blød	Soft shoulders
Udkørsel	Exit
Vejarbejde	Roadworks

driving licence	**førerbevis**
car registration papers	**registreringsattest**
green card	**grønt kort**
Can I park here?	**Må jeg parkere her?**
Are we on the right road for…?	**Er dette vejen til…?**
Fill the tank, please…	**Vær venlig at fylde op med…**
normal/super/unleaded	**almindelig/super/blyfri**
Check the oil/tyres/battery, please.	**Vær venlig at kontrollere olien/dækkene/batteriet.**
I've had a breakdown.	**Vognen er gået i stykker.**
There's been an accident.	**Der er sket en ulykke.**

D

DRUGS *(narkotika)*. Drugs are banned, and shouldn't be possessed in any form. Buyers or sellers of even soft drugs will be arrested and taken to police headquarters. Hard drug offenders of any sort are certain to be imprisoned. The normally courteous police are very firm on such matters.

DRUGSTORES—see **MEDICAL CARE**

ELECTRIC CURRENT. The standard voltage is 220, but some camping sites have this and 110. Plugs and sockets are different from both British and American types, but ask your hotel receptionist who might have an adaptor to spare.

E

EMBASSIES and CONSULATES *(ambassade; konsulat)*

Australia (embassy): Kristianiagade 21, 2100 Copenhagen Ø; tel.: 31 26 22 44

Canada (embassy): Kr. Bernikowsgade 1, 1105 Copenhagen K; tel.: 33 12 22 99

Eire (embassy): Østbanegade 21, 2100 Copenhagen Ø; tel.: 31 42 32 33

South Africa (consulate): Møntergade 1, 1116 Copenhagen K; tel.: 33 14 66 44

United Kingdom (embassy and consulate): Kastelsvej 36–40, 2100 Copenhagen Ø; tel.: 31 26 46 00

U.S.A. (embassy and consulate): Dag Hammarskjölds Allé 24, 2100 Copenhagen Ø; tel.: 31 42 31 44

E **EMERGENCY.** The all-purpose emergency number is 000, and called from public phone boxes it's free—coins are not needed. Ask for police, fire or ambulance as required. Speak distinctly (English will be understood) and state your number and location.

Emergency service *(skadestue),* in central Copenhagen—for accidents only, day and night:

Kommunehospitalet, Øster Farimagsgade 5, and
Rigshospitalet, Blegdamsvej 9 and Tagensvej 20

Doctor-on-call *(lægevagt):* in Copenhagen, ring 0041 around the clock for information.

Dental emergency: Tandlægevagten, Oslo Plads 14 (no phone calls), is open year round, 8–9.30 p.m. daily, on Saturdays, Sundays and public holidays also 10 a.m. to noon. Cash payment only.

ENTRY FORMALITIES. See also CUSTOMS CONTROLS and DRIVING. Most visitors—including citizens of Great Britain, the U.S.A., Canada, Eire, Australia and New Zealand—need only to possess a valid passport to enter Denmark. British subjects can enter on the simplified Visitor's Passport. You are generally entitled to stay in Denmark for up to three months without a visa. (This period includes the total time spent in Denmark, Finland, Iceland, Norway and Sweden in any six-month period.)

G **GUIDES and INTERPRETERS** *(guide; tolk).* Sightseeing tour buses and some canal boats will be accompanied by a multi-lingual guide. For special guide or interpreter service, call the Tourist Information Office at 33 11 13 25.

H **HAIRDRESSERS'** *(frisørsalon).* Rates reflect the variety of possibilities open, from the local to the trendy. Most major hotels have their own salons, but in any case the hotel receptionist will recommend a favourite place nearby. Tipping is unnecessary.

haircut	**klipning**
shampoo and set	**vask og vandondulation**
shampoo and blow-dry	**vask og føntørring**
permanent wave	**permanent**
dye/tint	**farvning/toning**

HITCH-HIKING. Thumbing a lift *(rejse på tommelfingeren)* is a well engrained practice, and you shouldn't have to wait too long.

Can you give me a lift to…?   **Må jeg køre med til…?**

HOTELS and ACCOMMODATION *(hotel; indlogering)*. See also CAMPING and YOUTH HOSTELS. Danish tourist offices will provide you with extensive lists of hotels and pensions. There is no star-system of rating, but the lists give an indication of various facilities (with or without bath, restaurant, number of beds, etc.). Combine this information with the prices listed, and you get a fair indication of quality. Ask your tourist office, too, for special low rates in off-season. They can be down by as much as 50 per cent.

At peak holiday periods, Copenhagen can be bursting at the seams with visitors, but the Accommodation Bureau, Kiosk P, at the Central Railway Station rarely fails to find room for all. The bureau is open daily from 9 a.m. to midnight between May 1 and September 15, and till 5 or 10 p.m. in off-season months. Application here must be made personally after your arrival.

Rates on page 104 are averages for double rooms in high season. Service charges and taxes are included. Single rooms, when available, are about 30–40 per cent cheaper.

"Mission Hotels" *(missionshotel)* are reasonably priced and popular with Danish family visitors. They are classified as temperance hotels, but will sell wine and beer to guests. For the motorist, there are motels all around Copenhagen, but a stay at a nearby village *kro* (country inn) can be a more novel experience. These usually small, former stagecoach inns combine good personal service with wholesome food. Boarding houses *(pensionat)* and private rooms can be booked through the Accommodation Bureau.

A hearty Danish breakfast is usually included in overnight rates, except at the most expensive hotels.

LANGUAGE. English is very widely spoken and understood: you can mostly get by with little else. Danish is perhaps the most difficult northern European language for relating the written word to speech; it's almost impossible to pronounce simply by reading the words, as many syllables are swallowed rather than spoken. Thus the island of Amager becomes *Am-air*, with the "g" disappearing, but in a distinctive Danish way difficult for the visitor to imitate. The letter "d" becomes something like a "th", but with the tongue placed behind the lower teeth, not the upper. The letter "ø" is like the "u" in English n*u*rse, but spoken with the lips far forward. And the letter "r" is again swallowed.

L There are 29 letters in the Danish alphabet—the 26 "normal", plus "æ" (as in egg), "ø", and "å" (as in port). They appear *after* the usual 26 (a point to remember when looking up names in phone books and lists).

Good morning	**Godmorgen**	Please/Thank you	**Vær så venlig/Tak**
Good afternoon	**Goddag**	You're welcome	**Ingen årsag**
Good evening	**Godaften**	Goodbye/See you soon	**Farvel/På gensyn**

Do you speak English? **Taler De engelsk?**

The Berlitz phrase book, DANISH FOR TRAVELLERS, covers practically all situations you're likely to encounter in your travels in Denmark, and the Danish–English/English–Danish pocket dictionary contains some 12,500 concepts, and a special menu-reader supplement, that will help over the worst stumbling blocks.

LAUNDRY and DRY CLEANING *(vask; kemisk rensning).* The large hotels offer same-day service, but not on weekends and holidays—and it's expensive. Dry cleaners are found throughout the city and are entered in the directory to trade and professions *(Fagbog)* under *Renserier.* You'll note that prices in launderettes *(selvbetjeningsvaskeri)* are more advantageous however, and these are open till late at night.

When will it be ready? **Hvornår er det færdigt?**
I must have this for tomorrow morning. **Jeg skal bruge det i morgen tidlig.**

LOST PROPERTY *(hittegods).* The general lost-property office *(hit-tegodskontor)* is at the police station in Carl Jacobsens Vej 20, open Monday to Friday from 10 a.m. to 3 p.m. (Thursdays till 5 p.m.) and closed Saturdays and Sundays. For property lost in buses, go to the Town Hall from Monday to Friday, 6 a.m. to 6 p.m., Saturday 10 a.m. to 2 p.m., or call 33 14 74 48. If you've forgotten anything in a train, the place to go is the Central Station, open from 10 a.m. to 6 p.m., Monday to Friday.

M **MAIL** *(post).* See also POST OFFICES. You can pick up your poste-restante (general-delivery) mail at the head post office at Tietgensgade 35 (just behind Tivoli) from 9 a.m. to 7 p.m., Monday to Friday, and Saturdays from 9 a.m. to 1 p.m., but not on Sundays. Identification is necessary.

Have your poste-restante mail addressed this way:

> Name
> Poste Restante
> Tietgensgade 35
> 1704 Copenhagen V
> Denmark

MAPS. Road maps *(vejkort)* of Denmark are on sale at filling stations and bookshops, and street plans *(bykort)* of the different cities and towns are handed out by tourist offices or can be picked up free in hotels. A map obtainable free from Huset ("Use It", see p. 31) is particularly useful, showing as it does all bus routes and youth hostels. The municipal bus company also produces a most useful map *(trafik-kort)* showing all roads and bus and S-train lines in Copenhagen and Zealand, with individual insets for main towns. The maps in this book are by Falk-Verlag, Hamburg, that also publish a detailed street plan of Copenhagen and a road map of Denmark.

a street plan of Copenhagen	**et bykort over København**
a road map of this region	**et vejkort over denne egn**

MEDICAL CARE. See also EMERGENCIES. To be at ease, make sure your health insurance policy covers any illness or accident while on holiday. Your travel agent or insurance company at home will be able to advise you.

In Denmark, treatment and even hospitalization is free for any tourist taken suddenly ill or involved in an accident. For minor treatments, doctors, dentists and chemists will charge on the spot. For EEC employees or pensioners and their families, however, this money will be partly refunded at the local Danish health service office (tourist bureaux will tell you where to go) on production of bills and the EEC Form E-111. Generally speaking, it's wise to enquire before departure about possible reciprocal health agreements and any forms needed.

A Danish chemist's *(apotek)* is not like a drugstore selling a wide range of pure medical and vaguely medical products, but strictly a dispensary. Some medicines which can be bought over the counter in other countries are available only on prescription. Pharmacies are listed in the trade phone book under *Apoteker*. Normal hours are from 9 a.m. to 5.30 p.m. An all-night service operates at Steno Apotek, Vester-brogade 6C, tel.: 33 14 82 66.

I need a doctor/dentist.	**Jeg har brug for en læge/tandlæge.**

M   **MEETING PEOPLE.** The Danes are happy to try their English on visitors, and it's easy to strike up a conversation in cafés and at tourist spots. They are the most easily approachable as well as the least formal of all Scandinavians, but a handshake on meeting and departure is recognized practice. A pleasantly affable *goddag* ("good day"—pronounced almost as in English) is much appreciated, as is *farvel* ("farewell" or "goodbye", pronounced far-VELL).

N   **NEWSPAPERS and MAGAZINES** *(avis; ugeblad).* You'll find English-language newspapers and magazines without any trouble at news-stands, shops and hotels throughout central Copenhagen. London papers arrive in the early morning, and for Americans in particular, there's the *International Herald Tribune.* A free English-language brochure, *Copenhagen This Week,* lists information for visitors.

Have you any English-language newspapers?   **Har De engelsksprogede aviser?**

P   **PETS and VETS.** Dogs and cats may be brought into Denmark without excess formalities. Dogs from rabies-free countries need no veterinary certificates from the country of origin. The practice at Copenhagen Airport is to send for a vet anyway to examine the animal, for which a fee is demanded. Clearance takes little more than an hour. For importing other animals, you'll need a special permit—consult in such cases a Danish consulate.

There are several animal clinics in Copenhagen, listed under *Dyrehospitaler* in the trades directory. Vets are listed under *Dyrlæger,* and there's even an animal ambulance *(dyreambulance)* offering a 24-hour service.

Unobtrusive dogs are generally welcomed in hotels. Owners are liable to be fined if their pet fouls the pavement; there are special "dog-toilets" in the parks.

PHOTOGRAPHY. Film is relatively inexpensive, so it's not worth bringing a stock from home. Developing and printing are of a high quality and can be done quickly, even in one hour, in central Copenhagen.

I'd like a film for this camera.   **Jeg vil gerne have en film til dette apparat.**

a black-and-white film	**en sort-hvid film**
colour prints	**en farvefilm**
colour slides	**en film til lysbilleder**
How long will it take to develop (and print) this film?	**Hvor lang tid tager det at fremkalde (og kopiere) denne film?**
May I take a picture?	**Må jeg tage et billede?**

POLICE. State and city police all form part of the national force and are dressed in black uniforms. Some walk their beat through central Copenhagen, but most policemen patrol in deep-blue-and-white or white cars with the word POLITI in large letters (although they also tend to roam around in indistinguishable unmarked cars). You're entitled to stop police cars at any time and request help. Police are courteous and speak English (they take a mandatory 80 English lessons during training).

Don't hesitate to go to the local police station if in need of advice. All are listed in the phone book under *Politi*. See also EMERGENCIES.

| Where's the nearest police station? | **Hvor er den nærmeste politi-station?** |

POST OFFICES and TELEGRAMS *(postkontor; telegram).* The main post office is in Tietgensgade (see MAIL for opening hours), and there are many sub-offices around town. All display a red sign with a crown, bugle and crossed arrows in yellow—and a sign saying "Kongelig Post og Telegraf". Stamp machines usually take two 1-krone pieces. When buying postcards from stands and souvenir shops, you can get the appropriate stamps on the spot. Danish postboxes, bright red, stand out cheerfully, as do the postmen—colourful characters in red uniforms riding yellow cycles.

Telegrams: All post offices handle telegrams; after hours, call 0022. The operator usually speaks English if necessary—but be particularly precise in your request. To avoid all chance of an important word being misspelt over the phone, go personally with your message to the main telegraph office *(telegrafkontor)* at Købmagergade 37, open daily from 9 a.m. to 10 p.m. See also TELEPHONE.

| A stamp for this letter/postcard, please. | **Et frimærke til dette brev/ postkort, tak.** |

PRICES. See page 104 for some average rates and the going prices. All cafés and restaurants have a menu displayed outside, so you can check **119**

P on prices before entering. To keep costs down, the plain advice is: eat around the university area and don't drink much anywhere! Eating out at lunchtime *al fresco* with *smørrebrød* purchased from a sandwich shop will also save kroner.

If seeking nightlife, take advice from your hotel receptionist on what you can expect to pay. Prices are so erratic you might save a small fortune this way.

The Danish VAT, or sales tax, called MOMS, is 22 per cent. It's always included in the bill. If you make any expensive buys, the tax can be reclaimed. Retailers accustomed to dealing with tourists are acquainted with the necessary procedures and can supply you with a "How to shop tax-free in Denmark" brochure.

Danes round off the bill, up or down, to the closest amount possible divisible by 25 øre because there are no intermediate coins (e.g. 13 is rounded off to 25, etc.).

PUBLIC HOLIDAYS *(fest-/helligdag)*. Though Denmark's banks, offices and major shops close on public holidays, museums and tourist attractions will be open, if on reduced Sunday hours. It will also be business as usual in the cafés.

January 1	*Nytår*	New Year's Day
June 5	*Grundlovsdag*	Constitution Day (half day)
December 25/26	*Jul*	Christmas
Movable dates:	*Skærtorsdag*	Maundy Thursday
	Langfredag	Good Friday
	Anden påskedag	Easter Monday
	Bededag	General Prayer Day (fourth Friday after Easter)
	Kristi himmelfartsdag	Ascension Day
	Anden pinsedag	Whit Monday

Are you open tomorrow?   **Har De åbent i morgen?**

PUBLIC TRANSPORT. An excellent public-transport system of frequent buses *(bus)* and underground trains *(S-tog)* starts weekdays at 5 a.m. and Sundays at 6 a.m. Last services leave the city centre at

12.30 a.m. Buses continue then to run on a skeleton service till late at night. For bus information, call 33 95 17 01; for S-train information, 33 14 17 01 (Central Station).

Tickets. The fare system in Copenhagen is somewhat complicated. It is valid for the HT-area—the city and surrounding region of 50 km.—which has been split into zones. Tickets entitle you to travel and transfer within a zone and to bordering zones for a limited period of time. Remember that tickets are interchangeable on buses and trains, which begin like an underground railway in the central district and then emerge into daylight on the suburban network.

Purchase a flat fare ticket *(grundbillet)* for single rides within a zone and to bordering zones only. Additional tickets, available at an extra cost, are required if you travel beyond the basic ticket zone. The more advantageous ticket coupons *(rabatkort)* are valid for 10 rides in several zones. Yellow coupons are good for 3 zones, green ones for 6 zones and grey ones for all zones. They can be purchased at train stations or from bus drivers.

Enter by the front door, tell the driver your destination and he'll give you the right ticket. Don't forget to time-stamp your coupon aboard the bus or in the yellow, automatic machines on train platforms. Passengers without valid stamped tickets are liable to on-the-spot fines. Children under 4 travel free and from ages 4–12 at half fare.

RADIO and TV *(radio; fjernsyn)*. Danish radio has three channels—Radio 1 (on 90.8 MH VHF) for news and comment and classical music; channels 2 and 3 (96.5/93.9 MH) for local news, lighter music and entertainment. There's a news programme in English on Radio 3 at 8.15 a.m., Monday to Saturday.

BBC long-wave and world services and European-based American networks can easily be picked up.

The main television transmission is from 7.30 to 11.30 p.m. All films are shown in their original version with Danish sub-titles.

RELIGIOUS SERVICES *(gudstjeneste/messe)*. The Danish Church is Protestant (Evangelical Lutheran). Sunday services in English are held in the following Copenhagen places of worship:

Church of England: St. Alban's Anglican Episcopalian Church, Churchill-parken, Langelinie. Sunday morning service and Holy Communion.

R **The American Church of Copenhagen.** Interdenominational and International, Farvergade 27. Sunday morning service, followed by Coffee Fellowship.

Roman Catholic: Jesu Hjerte Kirke, Stenosgade 4. Sunday morning mass.

Jewish services are held in Hebrew in the Synagogue, Krystalgade 12, daily in the early morning and evening.

S **SIGHTSEEING.** Copenhagen Excursions and Vikingbus run official sightseeing excursions from May 1 to Sept. 15 with Rådhuspladsen as their starting point.

Of special interest are the Industrial Art Tours visiting factories of leading producers of applied art—china and silver. This tour normally takes about 2½ hours.

There are also guided walking tours of Copenhagen several times weekly, with an English-speaking guide.

Other ways of seeing the city include visits with English-speaking taxi-driver or guide, guided tours by limousine and sightseeing flights. You'll get detailed programmes and tickets from most travel agents and hotel receptionists. See also CANAL TOURS.

SUBWAY—see **PUBLIC TRANSPORT**

T **TAXI.** Plenty of taxis cruise the streets of Copenhagen, but in wet weather it's difficult to find a vacant one. They are recognized by a *Taxi* or *Taxa* sign. Tips are included in the meter price, but round the sum off upwards—if pleased with service. All cabs are radio-controlled; call 31 35 35 35/31 35 14 20—or for a mini-bus taxi, 31 39 35 35. Most drivers speak English.

Copenhagen with its suburbs extends for miles, so have a look at where your destination lies and check on the availability of the cheaper bus/train services before leaping into a cab.

TELEPHONE *(telefon).* See also POST OFFICES. Apart from public telephones in newspaper- and tobacco-kiosks, public boxes are green-painted glass affairs with the word TELEFON on top. Insert two 25-øre pieces for short local calls, and 1 krone or 5 for long-distance calls. But look out—unused coins are *not* returned, even if your number is engaged. So insert a minimum. The consolation is that you can call another number, or repeat the engaged number, until the time you've paid for runs out. Some telephone booths require the use of a card (a *Telet*), obtained from kiosks all over town.

For long-distance calls within Denmark, there are no area codes, just dial the 8-digit number of the person you want to call.

The main telegraph office at Købmagergade 37 is open for phone calls, telegrams and telex from 9 a.m. to 10 p.m. every day, and the Central Station post office till 10 p.m. on weekdays, 4 p.m. on Saturdays and 5 p.m. on Sundays and holidays.

Beware—telephoning from your hotel room can be an expensive business.

Some useful numbers:

Telephone Operation Enquiries:	0030
Directory Enquiries:	0033

TIME DIFFERENCES. Denmark sticks to Central European Time (GMT + 1) as does most of the Continent. In summer, the clock is put one hour ahead (GMT + 2), and the time differences look like this:

New York	London	**Copenhagen**	Jo'burg	Sydney	Auckland
7 a.m.	noon	1 p.m.	1 p.m.	9 p.m.	11 p.m.

What time is it, please?   **Undskyld, hvad er klokken?**

TIPPING. A non-existant problem since basically you don't give tips. Hotel and restaurant bills always include service; tip only if special services have been rendered. Railway porters charge fixed prices, and no need to tip hairdressers, taxi drivers, theatre or cinema ushers. Only in a very few cases is there an exception to the rule, as for instance, when you leave the odd krone tip for use of the washbasin and facilities in ladies' and men's toilets.

T **TOILETS.** Facilities are usually indicated by a pictograph; alternatively they are marked *WC, Toiletter, Damer/Herrer* (Ladies/Gentlemen) or just by *D/H*. There's no charge unless you see it clearly marked to the contrary.

Where are the toilets?	**Hvor er toilettet?**

TOURIST INFORMATION OFFICES *(turistinformation)*. Danish tourist offices are among the most helpful in the world, and are excellently geared to provide information and a range of first-class brochures.

Australia: The Danish Tourist Board, 60 Market Street, P.O. Box 4531, Melbourne, Vic. 3001.

Canada: The Danish Tourist Board, P.O. Box 115, Station "N", Toronto, Ont. M8V 3S4.

United Kingdom: The Danish Tourist Board, 169–173, Regent Street, London W1R 8PY; tel.: (01) 734-2637/8.

U.S.A.: Scandinavian National Tourist Offices, 655 Third Avenue, 18th floor, New York, NY 10017; tel.: (212) 949-2333.

Scandinavian Tourist Board, Denmark-Sweden, 150 North Michigan Avenue, Suite 2110, Chicago, IL 60601; tel.: (312) 899-1121.

Scandinavian Tourist Board, Denmark-Sweden, 8929 Wilshire Boulevard, Suite 300, Beverly Hills, CA 90211; tel.: (213) 854-1549.

All Danish cities and most small towns have their own tourist information office marked by a large letter **i** on a green background. The main information office is at

H. C. Andersens Boulevard 22, A 1553 Copenhagen V; tel.: 33 11 13 25.

Where's the tourist office?	**Hvor ligger turistbureauet?**

TRAINS *(tog)*. A comprehensive and punctual network dealing with 1,200 movements a day operates from Copenhagen Central Station.

The local electrified S-train serves most of the suburbs every 20 minutes (see PUBLIC TRANSPORT).

Regional or coast trains *(Kystbanerne)* are diesels and cover outer Zealand.

Intercity trains *(Intercity)* are the backbone of the Danish State Railways' *(DSB-Danske Statsbaner)* long-distance traffic; one leaves every hour for Jutland and vice versa, for instance. The whole train is shunted aboard the Great Belt ferry to Funen island (seat reservations are required for through-passengers; ring the Central Station at 33141701.

Long-distance trains *(Lyntog)*, "ultra-specials" running at up to 140 k.p.h., also serve the Jutland route and, like intercity trains, have buffet bars, plus phones for passengers' use (seat reservations are required).

International trains, usually referred to by name (e.g. *Vikingen* or *Øresundspilen* for Stockholm), link Copenhagen with most of Europe. They have sleeping cars and couchette coaches for night travel.

For special tickets, see page 103.

TRAVELLER'S CHEQUES—see **CREDIT CARDS**

UNDERGROUND—see **PUBLIC TRANSPORT**

WATER *(vand).* You can drink water without any qualms from the tap in Denmark. Home-produced mineral water, if you prefer it, is excellent.

A glass of water, please.   **Et glas vand, tak.**

YOUTH HOSTELS *(vandrerhjem).* Copenhagen is something of a mecca for the rucksack brigade. There are nine city youth hostels and student hotels to cater for the influx and to prevent sleeping rough in the parks, which is frowned upon. Youth hostels as such require a membership card issued by an organization affiliated to the International Youth Hostel Association. If you haven't such a card, obtain a guest card from Denmark's Youth Hostels (see below). Bed linen can be hired at the hostel (down bags are not permitted). There's no age limit. A full list of Denmark's 80 odd youth hostels is available from Danish Tourist Board offices abroad.

Danmarks Vandrerhjem (Denmark's Youth Hostels), Vesterbrogade 39, 1620 Copenhagen V

At a student hotel *(ungdomsherberg),* restrictions on night-time closure and so on are more relaxed.

For any problem specifically in the youth field, call in at Huset's ("Use It") downtown youth information centre at Rådhusstræde 13 (tel.: 33156518 and open from 10 a.m. to 8 p.m. daily from June to September; thereafter, shorter hours). See also page 31.

Index

An asterisk (*) next to a page number indicates a map reference. For the city's major streets, squares, parks, etc., look under the general heading, e.g. "Streets".

INDEX

128

Selection of Copenhagen Hotels and Restaurants

BERLITZ

Where do you start? Choosing a hotel or restaurant in a place you're not familiar with can be hard. We have made a selection of some of the best options in Copenhagen and environs.

Our criteria have been price and location. In the hotel section, for a double room with bath and breakfast, Higher-priced means above 1,500 kr., Medium-priced 900–1,500 kr., Lower-priced below 900 kr. Don't forget the Youth Hostel option for reasonably priced accommodation—far more broad and family-oriented than you would probably expect from the name. As to restaurants, for a meal consisting of a starter, a main course and a dessert, Higher-priced means above 300 kr., Medium-priced 175–300 kr., Lower-priced below 175 kr.

Special features, where applicable, plus regular closing days are also given.

Just about all restaurants serve *smørrebrød* in some form, with certain making a real speciality of it. One or two *smørrebrød* constitute a sizeable meal; Danes often choose a meal of *smørrebrød* as a practical and affordable lunch out.

The Tivoli Gardens, right in the centre of Copenhagen, have a wide variety of restaurants ranging from expensive to quite economic. You wouldn't go there necessarily *just* to eat (though you can eat very well) but to make a whole enjoyable evening of it, with plenty of atmosphere (illuminations, music, people-watching—all free of charge), it's ideal.

HOTELS

HIGHER-PRICED
(above 1,500 kr.)

d'Angleterre
Kongens Nytorv 34
1050 Copenhagen K
Tel. 33 12 00 95; fax 33 12 11 18
130 rooms. Classic luxury hotel.
Le Restaurant. La Brasserie.

Kong Frederik
Vester Voldgade 23–27
1552 Copenhagen V
Tel. 33 12 59 02; fax 33 93 59 01
110 rooms. Queens Garden
restaurant. Queens Pub.

71 Nyhavn Hotel
Nyhavn 71
1051 Copenhagen K
Tel. 33 11 85 85; fax 33 93 15 85
86 rooms. Former warehouse.
Small rooms. Pakhuskælderen and
Fyrskib 71 restaurants.

Palace
Rådhuspladsen 57
1550 Copenhagen V
Tel. 33 14 40 50; fax 33 14 52 79
152 rooms.

The Plaza
Bernstorffsgade 4
1577 Copenhagen V
Tel. 33 14 92 62; fax 33 93 93 62
96 rooms. Attractive library bar.
Flora Danica restaurant.

SAS Royal
Hammerichsgade 1
1611 Copenhagen V
Tel. 33 14 14 12; fax 33 14 14 21
265 rooms. View. Sauna. Summit
and Cafe Royal restaurants.

SAS Scandinavia
Amager Boulevard 70
2300 Copenhagen S
Tel. 33 11 23 24; fax 33 57 01 93
542 rooms. Top of Town restau-
rant with panoramic view. Indoor
swimming pool, sauna.

Sheraton
Vester Søgade 6
1601 Copenhagen V
Tel. 33 14 35 35; fax 33 32 12 23
471 rooms. View. Kings Court
and Felix restaurants.

MEDIUM-PRICED
(900–1,500 kr.)

Alexandra
H.C.Andersens Boulevard 8
1553 Copenhagen V
Tel. 33 14 22 00; fax 33 14 02 84
63 rooms.

Ascot
Studiestræde 57
1554 Copenhagen V
Tel. 33 12 60 00; fax 33 14 60 40
90 rooms. No restaurant.

Copenhagen Admiral
Toldbodgade 24–28
1253 Copenhagen K
Tel. 33 11 82 82; fax 33 32 55 42
366 rooms. Former warehouse.

Falkoner Hotel
Falkoner Alle 9
2000 Frederiksberg
Tel. 33 19 80 01; fax 33 87 11 91
149 rooms.

Grand Hotel
Vesterbrogade 9A
1620 Copenhagen V
Tel. 31 31 36 00; fax 31 31 33 50
140 rooms.

Komfort
Løngangsstræde 27
1468 Copenhagen K
Tel. 33 12 65 70; tlx. 16 488
189 rooms.

The Mayfair Hotel
Helgolandsgade 3
1653 Copenhagen V
Tel. 31 31 48 01; fax 31 23 96 86
110 rooms. No restaurant.

Hotel Neptun
Skt. Annæ Plads 18
1250 Copenhagen K
Tel. 33 13 89 00; fax 33 14 12 50
66 rooms.

Opera
Tordenskjoldsgade 15
1055 Copenhagen K
Tel. 33 12 15 19; fax 33 32 12 82
87 rooms. Den Kongelige restaurant.

Park
Jarmers Plads 3
1551 Copenhagen V
Tel. 33 13 30 00; fax 33 12 05 10
64 rooms.

Richmond
Vester Farimagsgade 33
1625 Copenhagen V
Tel. 33 12 33 66; fax 33 12 05 10
127 rooms. La Cocotte restaurant.

Savoy
Vesterbrogade 134
1620 Copenhagen V
Tel. 31 31 40 73; fax 31 31 31 37
67 rooms.

Triton
Helgolandsgade 7–11
1653 Copenhagen V
Tel. 31 31 32 66; fax 31 31 69 70
117 rooms.

Webers
Vesterbrogade 11B
1620 Copenhagen V
Tel. 31 31 14 32; fax 31 31 14 41
81 rooms.

Within easy reach

Hellerup Parkhotel
Strandvejen 203
2900 Hellerup
Tel. 31 62 40 44; fax 31 62 56 57
69 rooms.

Marienlyst
Nordre Strandvej 2
3000 Helsingør
Tel. 42 21 18 01; fax 42 21 21 11
141 rooms. Indoor swimming pool, beach, minigolf. Casino.

Marina
Vedbæk Strandvej 391
2950 Vedbæk
Tel. 42 89 17 11; fax 42 89 17 22
100 rooms.

Skovshoved Hotel
Strandvejen 267
2920 Charlottenlund
Tel. 33 64 00 28
20 rooms. Good cuisine.

LOWER-PRICED
(below 900 kr.)

Absalon
Helgolandsgade 15
1653 Copenhagen V
Tel. 31 24 23 11; tlx. 19 124
252 rooms.

Astoria
Banegårdspladsen 4
1570 Copenhagen V
Tel. 33 14 14 19; tlx. 16 319
91 rooms.

Avenue
Åboulevarden 29
1960 Frederiksberg C
Tel. 31 37 31 11; tlx. 16 654
58 rooms.

Carlton
Halmtorvet 14
1700 Copenhagen V
Tel. 31 21 25 51
60 rooms.

Centrum
Helgolandsgade 14
1653 Copenhagen V
Tel. 31 31 31 11
60 rooms.

Christian d. IV
Dronningens Tværgade 45
1302 Copenhagen K
Tel. 33 32 10 44; fax 33 32 07 06
42 rooms. No restaurant.

City
Peder Skramsgade 24
1054 Copenhagen K
Tel. 33 13 06 66; tlx. 19 258
84 rooms.

Cosmopole
Colbjørnsensgade 5–11
1652 Copenhagen V
Tel. 31 21 33 33; fax 31 31 33 99
203 rooms.

Danmark
Vester Voldgade 89
1552 Copenhagen V
Tel. 33 11 48 06; tlx. 15 518
51 rooms. No restaurant.

Excelsior
Colbjørnsensgade 4
1652 Copenhagen V
Tel. 31 24 50 85; fax 31 24 50 87
48 rooms.

Missionshotellet Hebron
Helgolandsgade 4
1653 Copenhagen V
Tel. 31 31 69 06; tlx. 27 416
90 rooms.

Kong Arthur
Nørre Søgade 11
1370 Copenhagen V
Tel. 33 11 12 12; fax 33 32 61 30
63 rooms.

Selandia
Helgolandsgade 12
1653 Copenhagen V
Tel. 31 31 46 10; tlx. 19 124
68 rooms.

Sophie Amalie Hotel
Sankt Annæ Plads 21
1250 Copenhagen K
Tel. 33 13 34 00; tlx. 15 815
117 rooms.

Within easy reach

Bel Air
Løjtegaardsvej 99
2770 Kastrup
Tel. 31 51 30 33; fax 31 50 41 31
173 rooms.

Eremitage
Lyngby Storcenter 62
2800 Lyngby
Tel. 42 88 77 00; fax 42 88 17 82
117 rooms.

RESTAURANTS

HIGHER-PRICED
(above 300 kr.)

La Crevette
Bernstorffsgade 5
1577 Copenhagen V
Tel. 33 14 68 47
In Tivoli Gardens. Fish and seafood. Outdoor dining. View. Open end April to early September.

Divan 1
Vesterbrogade 3
1620 Copenhagen V
Tel. 33 11 42 42
In Tivoli Gardens. Open end April to early September.

Divan 2
Vesterbrogade 3
1620 Copenhagen V
Tel. 33 12 51 51
In Tivoli Gardens. Outdoor dining. View. Open end April to early September.

Les Etoiles et une Rose
Dronningens Tværgade 43
1302 Copenhagen K
Tel. 33 15 05 54; tlx. 37 374
Good cuisine. Closed Sunday.

St. Gertruds Kloster
Hauser Plads 32
1127 Copenhagen K
Tel. 33 14 66 30
Old monastery. Large wine cellar.

Glacis – La Chacotte
Esplanaden 22
1263 Copenhagen K
Tel. 33 14 45 54
Closed Sunday.

Kong Hans
Vingårdsstræde 6
1070 Copenhagen K
Tel. 33 11 68 68
Good cuisine. Attractive vaulted restaurant. Closed Sunday, mid-July to mid-August.

Krogs Fiskerestaurang
Gammel Strand 38
1202 Copenhagen K
Tel. 33 15 89 15
Fish and seafood. Closed Sunday.

Café Lumskebugten
Esplanaden 21
1263 Copenhagen K
Tel. 33 15 60 29
Charming setting. Outdoor dining. Closed Sunday.

Den sorte Ravn
Nyhavn 14
1051 Copenhagen K
Tel. 33 13 12 33

Within easy reach

Den gule Cottage
Strandvejen 506
2930 Klampenborg
Tel. 31 64 06 91
Pleasant cottage by the sea. View.
Reservation essential.

Søllerød Kro
Søllerødvej 35
2840 Holte
Tel. 42 80 25 05
Good cuisine. Pleasant restaurant
in 17th-century inn. Outdoor
dining.

MEDIUM-PRICED
(175–300 kr.)

A Hereford Beefstouw
Vesterbrogade 3
1620 Copenhagen V
Tel. 33 12 74 41
Closed Saturday and Sunday.

Baghuset
Gothersgade 13
1123 Copenhagen K
Tel. 33 12 32 61
Closed Sunday.

Bourgogne
Dronningens Tværgade 2
1302 Copenhagen K
Tel. 33 12 03 17
Closed Sunday and June to
mid-August.

Copenhagen Corner
Rådhuspladsen
1550 Copenhagen V
Tel. 33 91 45 45

Egoisten
Hovedvagtsgade 12
1103 Copenhagen K
Tel. 33 12 79 71
Closed Sunday.

Els
St. Strandstræde 3
1255 Copenhagen K
Tel. 33 14 13 41
Original 19th-century decor.

Leonore Christine
Nyhavn 9
1051 Copenhagen K
Tel. 33 13 50 40
Closed Sunday.

Miss Mess
Ny Østergade 21
1101 Copenhagen K
Tel. 33 12 64 80

Nouvelle
Gammel Strand 34
1202 Copenhagen K
Tel. 33 13 50 18
Closed Sunday.

Le Pavé
Gråbrødretorv 14
1154 Copenhagen K
Tel. 33 13 47 45
Closed Sunday.

Peder Oxe
Gråbrødretorv 11
1154 Copenhagen K
Tel. 33 11 00 77

Spinderokken
Trommelsalen 5
1614 Copenhagen V
Tel. 31 22 13 14

Within easy reach

Dragør Kro/Hotel
2791 Strandgade 30
Dragør 2791
Tel. 31 53 01 87

Marco Polo
Engvej 171
2300 Copenhagen/Amager
Tel. 31 55 14 33

Strandmøllekroen
Strandvejen 808
2930 Klampenborg
Tel. 31 63 01 04

LOWER-PRICED
(below 175 kr.)

Bøf & Ost
Gråbrødretorv 13
1154 Copenhagen K
Tel. 33 11 99 11
Closed Sunday.

Det lille Apotek
Store Kannikestræde 15
1169 Copenhagen K
Tel. 33 12 56 06
Inn since 1720. Old Copenhagen atmosphere.

Krasnapolsky
Vestergade 10
1456 Copenhagen K
Tel. 33 32 88 00

Lille Lækkerbisken
Gammel Strand 34
1202 Copenhagen K
Tel. 33 32 04 00
Lunch only.

Restaurant Ida Davidsen
St. Kongensgade 70
1264 Copenhagen K
Tel. 33 91 36 55
*Classic smørrebrød restaurant.
Lunch only. Closed Saturday
and Sunday.*

Sorgenfri
Brolæggerstræde 8
1211 Copenhagen K
Tel. 33 11 58 80
*Genuine Copenhagen smørrebrød
restaurant.*

Spisehuset
Rådhusstræde 13
1466 Copenhagen K
Tel. 33 14 52 70

Tokanten
Vandkunsten 1
1467 Copenhagen K
Tel. 33 91 19 18

Within easy reach

Bakkens Perle
Dyrehavsbakken
2930 Klampenborg
Tel. 31 64 31 64

Studenterkilden
Enghavevej 16
2930 Klampenborg
Tel. 31 64 40 95